Babies in the Rain

Also by Jeff A. Johnson

Do-It-Yourself Early Learning

Everyday Early Learning

Finding Your Smile Again

babies in the rain

Promoting Play, Exploration, and Discovery with Infants and Toddlers

JEFF A. JOHNSON

Redleaf Press®
www.redleafpress.org
800-423-8309

Published by Redleaf Press
10 Yorkton Court
St. Paul, MN 55117
www.redleafpress.org

First edition 2010
Cover design by Elizabeth Berry
Cover photograph by Jeff A. Johnson
Interior typeset in Minion and Eurostile
Interior photos by Jeff A. Johnson
Developmental edit by Beth Wallace
Printed in the United States of America
16 15 14 13 12 11 10 09   1 2 3 4 5 6 7 8

Library of Congress Cataloging-in-Publication Data

Johnson, Jeff A., 1969–
  Babies in the rain : promoting play, exploration, and discovery with infants and toddlers / Jeff A. Johnson. — 1st ed.
     p. cm.
  Includes bibliographical references.
  ISBN 978-1-933653-84-6 (alk. paper)
  1. Infants. 2. Learning. 3. Infants—Care. 4. Infants—Development. I. Title.
HQ774.J63 2009
649'.122—dc22
                           2009001047

Printed on acid-free paper

To Tyler and Zoë

Being your dad is the proudest
accomplishment of my life.
Watching you play, explore, and discover the world
for yourselves as infants and toddlers was fascinating.
Thanks for teaching me.

Contents

Foreword

Babies in the rain" is an evocative image. For me it conjures up a toddler's delight in splashing in puddles, squishing mud, and reaching out to catch the falling drops. It's the newness of spring—and of the toddler's discoveries. It's the wonder in his eyes when that first drop lands on his nose, when he figures out how to make a big splash, or when he watches a leaf being sucked down a storm drain. And it's that same joy and wonder reflected on the face of parent or caregiver who loves the child and delights in her accomplishments and discoveries.

In Jeff Johnson's skillful narrative, you'll meet a bevy of delightful babies. You'll laugh—and sometimes wince—at their innocent antics as they play, explore, discover, struggle with problems of their own making, and reach out for comfort and affirmation. You'll tune in to the simple pleasures of watching a child take her first steps, stare entranced at a grass-hopper, or gently comfort a friend in distress. If you haven't spent time with a baby for a while, you'll relive the magic of being "in the moment" with a young child, intensely focused on the "dance" between you as the two of you engage in the back-and-forth serve-and-return interactions that build her brain and cement your attachment to each other.

As Jeff Johnson points out, "Babies belong in the rain"—at least when that rain is gentle and warm. They need many, many opportunities every day to explore the world with all of their senses and all of the motion, curiosity, and adventurousness they can muster. And they need adults by their sides who can help them to safely explore that world and discover how it works.

Babies also belong in a metaphorical rain. They need to float in a nurturing emotional environment, where a network of parents, extended family, caregivers, and older children shower them with respect and affection. They need stable, long-term relationships so that those who care for them have learned to respond to their individual ways of engaging with people and expressing their wants and needs.

Babies also need to be bathed in rich, engaging, natural language. The more words they hear—spoken directly to them in ways that capture their interest and encourage their response—the more they will learn. The more words they learn and the more practice they get in using those words to ask questions, tell stories, exchange information, and influence others' behavior, the faster their language and learning will grow. As their language becomes richer and more sophisticated, they will get more and more opportunities to learn from peers and adults, to engage others as play partners, and—eventually—to learn to read. A rich language foundation gives children an ongoing and increasing advantage in both social-emotional and intellectual development. It primes them to succeed in school and to enjoy self-chosen learning pursuits. And for children who are fortunate enough to learn two or more languages in early childhood, that foundation can lead to an even richer set of experiences.

Adults who do a lot of talking with babies—right from the start—tend to persist in these patterns. They use language to play with babies and toddlers. They sing soothing lullabies and happy, upbeat nursery songs. They talk about what they are thinking, doing, and feeling—or what the baby is doing and how she might be feeling. They respond to babies' overtures, capitalize on their interests, and engage their attention. They get babies to coo, laugh, babble, and eventually talk back.

In the busy social world of a high-quality child care setting like the one Jeff Johnson describes, babies and toddlers are showered with a wealth of words. Adults respond to their cues and overtures, using words and nonverbal communications to provide comfort, predictability, explanation, guidance, and affirmation as needed. Group activities and adventures provide opportunities to sing songs, follow simple directions, and learn new words. Older children introduce all kinds of specific vocabulary as they engage babies in their imaginative play routines and direct them in roles such as beauty parlor customer, patient, and copilot. Beautiful books are readily available, as are readers willing to share favorites over and over again, naming pictures, retelling the story, and engaging a toddler's enthusiastic participation.

In such rich surroundings, with so many opportunities for meaningful communication, babies' language flourishes. Soon they, too, are asking interesting questions, telling real and fanciful stories, repeating silly rhymes and fun phrases, singing songs, making jokes, and making their desires known in no uncertain terms. They use their words to make requests, negotiate conflicts, express feelings, guide their own behavior, and engage others in play.

At a more abstract level, babies need protection from the incessant rain of noise, bright lights, media messages, and stress that falls on all of us in today's world. Here Jeff Johnson minces no words. His own experiences as a parent and as a child care provider have underscored what recent research confirms:

- Babies thrive on moderate amounts of stimulation, especially when they can control it by making an exciting thing happen again and again. But too much stimulation is overwhelming and causes them to shut down.

- Babies pick up on adult stress. Whether an adult is distant and distracted, tense and frustrated, or even angry or abusive—babies bear the brunt. Chronic stress can be "toxic" to developing brain circuits. It floods the brain with chemicals that can interfere with a baby's ability to learn. It can also set the brain's threshold for responding to dangers too high or too low—so that minor intrusions are treated as immanent threats or urgent commands are ignored until they escalate into abuse.

- Babies need adults to help them handle everyday challenges and more serious stressors. An adult's reassuring presence and calming voice and manner buffers the mild stress of a minor tumble or the frustration of not being able to get a block into its hole—or the more severe stress of an inoculation, an absent parent, or a serious illness or hospitalization.

- TV and videos—even "educational" ones—are not healthy for children under two. Indeed, too much early screen time can retard their language development and lead to later problems with paying attention, resisting distraction, and completing tasks.

- Babies are naturally curious. They are driven to explore, to learn, and to practice new skills. They need constant, safe opportunities to move about and try things for themselves—with adults available to steer them away from danger and support and celebrate their successes.

- Too many babies today are not getting what they need. They are getting too much artificial stimulation from TV, computers, electronic toys, and rockers, and too little human interaction and conversation.

The problem isn't that parents don't care, or that they entrust their young children to people unconcerned for their welfare. Every parent has strengths, and most desperately want the best for their children and will work hard to ensure that they get it. And most people who care for babies for pay or as a favor to their parents do it at least in part out of love. But caring for a baby—and especially for a group of young children—is an ever-changing challenge. Babies cry—sometimes incessantly and for no reason that an adult can find and fix. Toddlers test limits, insist on their own way, and get into all kinds of troubles that can be difficult to predict. Two-year-olds imitate inappropriate behavior, throw tantrums, and sometimes play with such intensity and determination that nothing but a meltdown will stop them. The pressures of the adult world add still more stress. When support, knowledge, and other adults to turn to for backup are limited, the quality of care can suffer. In the United States today, infant/toddler child care is so underfunded and undersupported that inadequate quality is all too common.

A host of studies in the past twenty years have reported serious deficits in the quality of care that infants and toddlers are likely to receive. Some of these studies have also highlighted an important predictor of good quality—the caregiver's *intentionality*. Intentional caregivers

- deliberately *choose* to care for and teach young children

- think of this work as a profession, calling, or enjoyable and rewarding occupation

- seek out information, resources, and supports to help them do a good job

- reflect on how each day went and talk with children's parents about their child's needs, feelings, and accomplishments

- set up the environment and plan activities with purpose

- seize and delight in the "teachable moments" when a child's interest or question or behavior provides them with an opening to expand the child's knowledge or reinforce an important value.

Intentional caregivers make good choices for babies.

Making good choices for babies means following your head, heart, and gut. It means doing your best each day to meet the needs of children in your care, to shower them with love, respect, and rich brain-building language. It means noticing what intrigues them and setting up opportunities for them to master the challenges they set for themselves as they play, explore, and discover a world of friendships, natural wonders, and beautifully crafted books. It means getting to know each child well so you can answer her questions, enrich her play, and enjoy learning together. It means letting children help in whatever ways they can and giving them just enough help to enable them to master new skills.

Making good choices for babies also requires a longer view. It means making healthy choices to turn off the TV, lower your stress, turn down the barrage of overstimulating attention grabbers and sales pitches, eat wholesome food, buy less, and play more. It means seeking out information on child development and early education and finding resources in your community that can enhance children's learning. It means thinking about the values that you want to pass on, sharing stories that embody those values, and creating routines and rituals that enable children to learn and practice positive behaviors. It means intentionally strengthening the web of relationships that enables each child to flourish.

Finally, making good choices for babies means playing an active role in shaping the world in which they are growing. It means supporting child care providers so that they can support young children. It means working to improve their pay and working conditions and to ensure that they get the education, respect, and collegial support they need to do their jobs well. It means joining with others to advocate for policies that protect all babies and facilitate their optimal development. It means asking questions of your elected representatives and of candidates for office. It means voting in the interest of babies and urging others to do the same.

For grown-ups who care about babies, *Babies in the Rain* is both reassuring and provocative. It is not the sort of book you save to savor on a rainy day. Rather, it is a practical, fun-to-read guide that you'll want to dip into again and again—especially if you spend time with an infant or toddler. And—like your memories of mud pies and warm spring rains—it's a treasure that you'll want to share, especially with those who share in the caring of children you love.

—Betty Bardige, Ed.D
author of *Talk to Me, Baby!*

≡☆
Acknowledgments

First off, this book would not have been possible without the support of Tasha, my one true love. She did not roll her eyes at me when I said, "I have a new book idea; Redleaf wants to publish it," or "I have to go write," and she helped me survive and overcome my first bout with writer's block. Thank you.

Thanks also to Tyler, Zoë, Siddha, Annie, Lilly, Brenden, Marygrace, Phoebe, Ty, Sam, Hunter, Maddie, Kada, Adrian, Brooke, and all the other infants and toddlers I have known over the years. Watching them learn to know the world made this book possible.

Thanks to Beth Wallace for her willingness to edit another one of my books. The structure, flow, and content all work better thanks to her.

The hard work of the dedicated people at Redleaf Press needs acknowledgment too. Linda Hein's work as publisher has reenergized and rejuvenated the Redleaf Press brand. Editors David Heath and Kyra Ostendorf helped refine ideas, provided direction, and gave support when I hit a wall halfway through the first draft. Thanks to the Redleaf production team: Douglas Schmitz, Laurie Herrmann, Laura Maki, Jim Handrigan, and Carla Valadez. Thanks to Jan Grover, Julie Maas, and Laura Weller, your hard work turned my rough manuscript files into this pretty little book. Special thanks to JoAnne Voltz and Inga Weberg, Redleaf's marketing manager and sales manager. Not many people would see this book if it were not for your hard work.

Introduction

Almost three-month-old Lilly lies on a cuddly green blanket, her Lilly pad, watching the action around her. Older children stop by to offer toys, read stories, sing songs, and marvel at her tiny fingers and toes. Her busy eyes watch the children as they move in and out of her line of sight. She also gazes at the gliding bursts of color in the nearby aquarium and the dance of sunlight from the windows across the room. Her arms and legs pump with exuberant joy, and she vocalizes her good spirits. Then, when she has had enough, when her busy mind and body are tired, her head drifts to the right, and she falls asleep.

....

Brenden has been in constant motion his entire life—a little more than a year. He rolled over, sat, stood, and walked earlier than average. He is usually headed somewhere in a hurry. He roars along, an irresistible force looking for an object to move. He loves to be outside. Like a puppy, a chocolate Lab or maybe a Saint Bernard, his ears perk up and he heads to the door when he sees someone put on her shoes. Outside, he is in four-wheel drive going over, under, or straight through anything in his path. "Around" is not in his vocabulary. Bumps, bruises, and scratches cover his body, like medals pinned to the chest of a great explorer. He slows down here and there to pick up a bit of nature—a small pine cone, an inviting stick, a clump of dirt, a handful of grass. He examines these treasures on the fly, maybe tasting them, usually casting them aside for something fresh that has caught his attention, some new bit of the world to know.

....

Marygrace, a brand-new two-year-old, sits on a small chair looking at a book. In front of the chair, her bare feet rub together in a small cardboard box; a well-used baby doll blanket drapes her shoulders. She does her best to obey orders from three-year-old Phoebe: "Sit still while I pump up the chair. Close your eyes so I can cut your bangs. Your toes are done soaking, let me paint your toenails. Tilt your head back; I need to wash your hair. Go look in the mirror; you're ready for the ball!" Marygrace is learning Beauty Shop and many other dramatic play scenarios from Phoebe. Over the last few weeks, her quickly growing vocabulary and her willingness to be bossed around a bit have transformed her from a pesky toddler into a viable playmate.

....

The *drip-drip-drip* of warm rain on his head and face call forth squeals of delight as Adrian's eyes widen and gleam; his legs and arms flap with joy. As soon as his hands and knees touch the deck, he ventures forward a foot or so, pausing to examine his wet fingers and then pound them against the surface. Fine droplets of water spray up each time Adrian's palms strike. His little brain is fully engaged in this moment as his senses relay information: the sight of a billion raindrops dancing in the spring breeze, the sound of their contact with the deck, the taste of the drops that hit his lips and tongue, the heady smell of wet grass and mulch drifting from the yard, the feel of the rain and breeze on his arms and legs. Adrian enjoyed heaps of time on his tummy at our house when he was younger, and now that he is mobile, he is a fervent explorer.

Crack! Lightning and then thunder fills the sky. Adrian lurches back into a sitting position and, lower lip quivering, repeatedly shifts his gaze from my eyes to the clouded sky. He sees that the sound and fury of the approaching storm have not alarmed me. We exchange smiles, and he returns to his gleeful splashing. After another incredible ten minutes or so, the storm intensifies, and we head back inside to a large, white, fluffy towel and some cuddle time.

....

Infants and toddlers are amazing. There is no other way to describe their innate drive to know the world they are born into; the speed at which they acquire, integrate, and use knowledge; their unique personalities; their rate of physical growth; and their astounding brains. From their very beginnings, Lilly, Brenden, Marygrace, and Adrian have been unfolding into incredibly different people with a vast array of likes, dislikes, interests, and personality quirks. Infants and toddlers are art, science, poetry, engineering, chemistry, and physics rolled into fascinatingly cute—and nearly helpless—little bundles. They are the past and future, carrying our genetic code and our civilization into an unknown world we will not experience. They are hope, opportunity, and possibility.

....

The Marvel of Infants and Toddlers

Babies are born explorers. Infants belong in the rain. They belong outside in the grass and dirt. They belong on the floor with materials that will engage their senses and minds—stimulating them but not overstimulating them the way too many of today's "educational" toys tend to do. They belong in the loving arms of calm, happy, focused caregivers who are in tune with children's needs. They belong in environments that promote developmentally appropriate play, exploration, and discovery. They belong in settings that look upon them as curious, thinking, contemplative, emotional, complex individuals. They belong on their tummies, bottoms, hands and knees, and finally their unstable feet as they get to know their world.

Many people miss this, thinking a baby is a baby is a baby, seeing them as interchangeable and indistinguishable until about the age of three, when they magically become people. They fail to look below the surface of dirty diapers, ear infections, 2:36 AM feedings, thick green snoterpillars, drool, messes, and expenses to see the wonderment of infanthood and toddlerhood. They miss the amazing.

Even people who see infants and toddlers as unique and remarkable entities often have a hard time understanding them. We all started out as infants, then toddlers, but even though we lived through it, we do not carry clear memories of how our minds and emotions worked in our earliest years. Since we don't remember our first years and cannot rely on memories of our experiences during that time, we have to depend on our observational skills to understand what is going on in minds like Brenden's, when he plows through shrubs and flower beds, or Marygrace's, when she plays with Phoebe.

For most of human civilization, the inner life and development of infants and toddlers did not receive much thought. Once adults started trying to understand them, the observational tools at hand—our senses—limited us. We tried comprehending what they understand through what we observed. Jean Piaget, Erik Erikson, Lev Vygotsky, Magda Gerber, Maria Montessori, and other pioneers were remarkable observers, but they could do only so much with the tools available to them. It was not until very recently that powerful computers and scanners made it possible to look unobtrusively inside young brains for a clearer picture of what makes infants and toddlers tick.

Giving Infants and Toddlers What They Need to Be Safe and Thrive

Much of what we *think* we know about infants and toddlers is wrong. By the time good research reaches parents and caregivers, it is dumbed down, snipped into bite-size video and audio clips, filtered, spun, sanitized, and packaged for consumption. On top of that, some research has predetermined results intended to drive a specific policy, product, or point of view. The reality is that not everyone investigating how the minds of infants and toddlers work has the best interests of those infants and toddlers in mind.

While letting infants and toddlers experience real rain is a good thing, the metaphorical rain we often leave them in is troubling. This blurred view of babies has led to a flood of mistaken, misguided, and misinformed thinking about infant and toddler development. It has led to clouded thinking and judgment. While I do not believe many people in our world are seeking intentionally to do infants and toddlers wrong, I do believe that numerous individuals, businesses, and public policies are unintentionally doing young children and their families wrong. They are spinning and twisting to present the reality that best fits their interests. A torrent of slick, calculated, and cunning marketing strategies seeps into the lives of families, permeating their choices in everything from diapers to cereal to minivans. I even checked with my editor to see if she would have a problem with me using the adjectives *greedy*, *myopic*, and *evil* to describe people who market products to and through infants and toddlers. As an editor, she felt the language was too combative, but as a parent, she did not disagree with it.

Infants and toddlers have become a new demographic to target, a new market segment to sell to, a new revenue stream to exploit. Marketers may not intend to harm families and children with these business practices, but it is happening nonetheless.

A deluge of well-intended public policies are missing the mark—or worse yet, ignoring it altogether. Making the politically correct choice, the easy choice, or the superficial choice has become standard operating procedure on both the Left and the Right. We live in a nation where most children receive at least some of their care in nonparental child care settings at a time when research shows that 80 percent of that care rates as either poor or mediocre (California Childcare Health Program 2006).

Loving parents feel the clear voice of reason drowned out by unrelenting pressure from marketers, government, and peers. Parents want to make the right choices for their children, but because of the muddiness of the information they receive, they don't know what right looks like. All the spin and questionable facts fed to parents by sources they think they should trust and respect cloud their intuition about what is best for their young children. In the end, this pressure leads to stress, tension, frustration, and anxiety, which their children sense and internalize.

At the same time, a push toward academics washes away age-appropriate, child-directed play, exploration, and discovery. These are replaced with so-called educational toys, television, lapware—computer software small children use while sitting on an adult's lap, DVDs, flash cards, prenatal learning devices, and other questionable gizmos. Drip by drip, we are draining away childhood from even the youngest children.

I had intended to start off this book as a rant against *them*. I wanted to shake my fist in the air, step up on my soapbox and wave my finger in indignation, jump up and down as I gave *them* a piece of my mind. I wanted to feel morally superior, turn up my nose, and enumerate all the wrongs committed by *them*. I wanted to perch in a tall tree on the high ground and look down on *them* in judgment.

Sadly, as best as I can tell, there are no *them*. There are no unknown corporate puppet masters controlling the intricacies of our lives, no clandestine government agencies influencing our choices in toothpaste and presidents, no unseen alien overlords running the show from another dimension. It would be easier to put responsibility for all those cold, wet babies on the skinny, gray-green shoulders of alien overlords, but we don't have that luxury. It's just individuals, each of us making our own choices as we go about living our lives. Realizing that we are responsible is a little overwhelming. It would be much easier to blame the current state of infanthood and toddlerhood on corrupt corporations, dim-witted politicians, and maniacal media moguls than to accept responsibility ourselves, but in the end the responsibility lies on our shoulders—we have to bring our babies in from that cold, harsh metaphorical rain where too many are forgotten.

Our Choices Influence the Lives of Infants and Toddlers

In the following chapters, we will take a clear look at these topics:

- What is really known about infant and toddler development

- The choices we are making in relation to infants and toddlers

- Building stronger emotional environments by focusing on mindful and in-the-moment interactions

- Promoting child-centered and age-appropriate learning through play, exploration, and discovery

- Encouraging language development from birth

Young children are capable, resourceful, and resilient, but we have to put more thought into the environments in which they develop. We have a choice. We can leave them out in that figurative rain, or we can make a change. This book provides tools to help you take more responsibility for your choices for infants and toddlers. You are one person and can't change the whole world, but you can change the choices you make. Even slightly better choices will mean happier, healthier, and better-cared-for infants and toddlers. If many readers choose to make better day-to-day choices—and if some of you influence your peers to do the same—we can generate big change in infant and toddler care. We don't have to be perfect, and we don't have to make all the right choices. We just have to be a bit more thoughtful and make slightly better choices more often. This is important stuff, but we are going to look at it through glasses tinted with hope and humor.

Engaging Infants' and Toddlers' Innate Drive to Play, Explore, and Discover

To do right by infants and toddlers as a society, we have to act mindfully. We have to act based on the big-picture outcomes we want to see. It is easy to talk about how much we care about children, how they are our future, and how we should not leave any of them behind. Talk is easy, but action is hard. Making good choices and then acting on them is the only way to bring about change.

Oh, and if I happen to be completely wrong about the alien overlords thing and they finally reveal themselves and their control over every aspect of our lives, the contents of this book will come in handy while we plot the rebellion to free humanity from their grasp. If that doesn't work, you can always throw it at their leader during the uprising. Aim for the soft spot right between his five big, yellow alien eyes.

Then again, we could just send four-wheel-drive Brenden out to get to know them.

Chapter 1

What's Going On in There?

I t's June 19, 1991, at 11:16 in the morning. My son, who will soon be named Tyler, was born sixty seconds ago. I am awestruck by his arrival—so small, so fragile, so perfect, so slimy, so loud. Tasha looked so beautiful; she had been so strong throughout a night of labor. I remember that we waited until after an episode of *Cheers* ended at 10:30 the night before to head to the hospital because she said there was no need to rush. I remember the doctor asking her to reposition herself— during a contraction—and how she told him in no uncertain terms that he would need to wait a while. I remember trying to be as strong and prepared as she was. I was there, trying to be supportive, but she did all the work.

I had been an adult for a while, but the moment of Tyler's birth was the moment I became a grown-up. I realized I was completely unprepared *and* up to the challenge in the same moment. I realized our planning for his arrival was insufficient *and* that it really did not matter—things would be okay. I realized all the preparation in the world cannot prepare you to be a parent. What prepares you to be a parent is the first look in your first child's eyes. A room that had moments before been full of pushing and noise was now calm. His dark eyes pierced my heart and changed my life.

In my experience, there are very few single moments you can look back on in life and say, "That changed me." Most life change happens gradually, not in a flash of insight and awareness. This was one of those rare change-in-a-flash-of-light moments. His birth not only called forth my hidden potential but also called forth my desire to live up to that potential. I was a dad. We were a family. I was up to the task—we were up to the task. Things would be okay.

The only problem was that as perfect as he was on the outside, as resolved as I was to do what was right for him, I had no idea what right really looked like. I wanted to make the best choices possible, choices to assure his health, happiness, and well-being in the short and long term. He had a beautiful little head I could not stop looking at, a head full of potential, but I had no idea what was going on in there.

Over the last twenty years working with young children, I have had many opportunities to wonder what is going on in their busy little heads:

Hunter, nearly three years old, has been sitting on the toilet trying to poop for five minutes or so. His skinny arms strain to support his weight. He fidgets, twists from side to side, and hums a happy tune. After a bit, a serious look overtakes him, and his constant motion stops. In the blink of an eye, he reaches one hand between his legs and exclaims, "Look, I can poop on my hand!"

. . . .

Siddha, not quite two years old, is upset because someone on the other side of the room has picked up a toy she feels is hers. Her hands are balled into tight little fists at her sides and her teeth are clenched and showing. Her usually wide eyes are now narrow slits. I think I see a bit of steam coming from her ears. If her skin was green and she was wearing ripped purple pants and a tattered shirt, she could pass as the baby version of the Incredible Hulk. Then, in half a second, her usual happy grin, dancing eyes, and peaceful demeanor reappear, and she toddles off to play.

Baby Bryce, happy on his tummy on the infant room floor, is mesmerized by the dance of sunshine and shadows on the wall opposite the window. A large, green, plastic block just out of his reach soon has his attention. As he twists and wiggles, the slowly spinning ceiling fan grabs his attention from the block. He cranes his neck, twists, twists further to improve his view, and all of a sudden flops onto his back. He is startled but happy with his new position. The fan holds his busy little brain captive for a few minutes until someone scoops him up without a word and hauls him to the changing table, where he promptly begins to cry.

....

The common thread connecting these scenes is a child's attempt at knowing the world. From their very beginnings, children seek meaning; they work to make sense of their world, to sort it into more refined categories, to know what they need to know to survive and thrive. They experiment to gain information and understanding of their physical and social worlds, to comprehend and expand their abilities, to develop tools for coping with varying situations and circumstances. An infant born into a household where English is the predominant language of daily life learns to speak English. An infant born into a household where Cantonese is the principal language develops the skills needed to speak Cantonese. An infant raised in an environment where American Sign Language is the primary language learns American Sign Language.

Ready to Learn from Birth

Infants and toddlers are born scientists, born explorers, born to learn what they need to know to succeed in the environment in which they find themselves. When you look at an infant or toddler and wonder, "What's going on in there?" the short answer to your question is *learning*.

When Hunter pooped on his hand, he was not trying to shock or upset me; he was performing an experiment to help himself better understand his world. It's hard to get inside the mind of a child, but he was probably thinking something like this:

• Am I able to poop on my hand?

- What is the texture and consistency of my poop?

- How will Jeff react if I poop on my hand?

- What is poop made of?

- How does my body make poop?

- Is my hand quick and agile enough to catch my poop before it hits the water?

- What color is my poop today?

- Does my poop look different in my hand than it does in the toilet?

- Why are we not supposed to pick up poop?

- What does poop taste like?

- Why do they hang the pictures I make on the wall but flush away the poop I make as soon as I make it?

In fact, he probably was unconsciously thinking many of those things at the same time he was working to master the whole poop-in-the-toilet-then-wipe-then-flush-then-pull-up-my-pants-then-wash-my-hands-then-close-the-bathroom-door-without-slamming-it scenario that we try to ingrain in the minds of young children. The point is that his action was an attempt to learn. There was a search for meaning behind his action, even if I didn't understand what he was thinking. Children's actions have meaning even if we do not understand them. While they may know the meaning of their actions, they probably do not appreciate them on a conscious level. So much of what happens in our brains happens behind the scenes, away from conscious acknowledgment.

The above list of poop-related thoughts probably grossed out some readers at least a little because, as adults, we think poop is icky and something not talked about in polite society. This highlights a huge difference between the way small children think and the way adults think. Children are new to the world and have not developed all the categories we adults have for classifying life as it unfolds. Infants and toddlers are figuratively and literally sorting out the world as they go about their little lives. Trying to figure out what fits where involves hands-on interaction with the world. Sometimes that means trying to force a doll shoe onto your foot, and sometimes it means pooping on your hand. Until they have a chance to learn for themselves, young children do not know that we touch *these* things and not *those* things, that we talk about *these* topics and avoid *those* topics, that we can say *these* things but *those* things are completely off-limits and may make Mom's jaw drop to the floor.

By the way, as I sit and write this, it's been four years since the scene in the bathroom with Hunter. It is very easy for me to talk now about his attempts to learn about the world around him, but in that moment I was shocked and upset—who poops on his own hand? His action caught me completely off guard and unprepared. This is a common problem for parents and caregivers, because our adult minds work so differently than their baby minds. We often expect them to know and understand the things we know and understand, and when they do not, we react with a mixture of anger and shock. Oh, and to my knowledge, Hunter never pooped on his hand again, so he must have learned what he needed to know.

The short answer to "What's going on in there?" is learning. The long answer—trying to figure out how that learning occurs and how we can support it—has required thousands of hours of research and filled many books over the last few decades, and there is still a lot we do not comprehend about what's happening inside those cute little heads. To understand better how that learning takes place, we are going to first look at what is going on in the very youngest brains and then look at what we need to know to help those busy baby brains really get what they need from the world around them.

Here are some basics about the form and function of an average infant or toddler brain:

- Infants come equipped with around 80 billion neurons. Neurons are brain cells—nerve cells that handle information processing. Neurons are made up of a cell body, an axon, and many dendrites.

- A neuron brings information in from other neurons through hair-like structures called dendrites.

- A neuron sends information out to other cells through a single axon.

- The dendrites and the axons meet at a synapse; this is where the actual exchange of information takes place. There are very few of these connections at birth, but this changes quickly. There are an estimated 1,000 trillion of these connections by the age of three. In the early years of life, each neuron will make up to 15,000 of these connections with other brain cells.

- The communication between cells that takes place at the synaptic terminals consists of a combination of chemical and electrical signals. The transmission of an electrical signal across a synaptic terminal requires a neurotransmitter chemical like serotonin, dopamine, or endorphins. These electrochemical signals jump small gaps between one cell's axon and another cell's dendrite.

- There are periods when young brains are most receptive to learning specific information. While these windows of learning opportunity are open wide at some points, they never completely close. Wide-open windows are prime times for learning.

- By the age of three, a child will have twice as many connections between neurons as Mommy or Daddy. In the second decade of life, the brain starts purposely pruning back the number of connections until they reach adult levels.

- Pruned connections were either unused or had inappropriately targeted connections. Connections that are activated repeatedly develop stronger signals. If these signals grow strong enough, they become exempt from elimination and survive into adulthood.

- Early experiences are a vital part of this process. They help make the connections and determine which ones are most used. Babies are born with brains ready to make the most of their environments.

- The pruning of synaptic connections is an important component of brain development because it allows the adult brain to process information quickly and efficiently.

In a nutshell, infants and toddlers learn through interactions with their environments. They use the input received from these interactions with the world to create many, many more connections between cells in their brains than will be needed in adulthood. Babies have brains wired to make the most of the world they encounter at birth. The strongest, most active connections will survive into adulthood, while pruning eliminates unused or poorly linked connections.

It's important for parents and caregivers to have a general idea of how early brain development works, but understanding detailed specifics is probably more than most people need—or want—to know. Infants and toddlers were surviving and thriving in their environments long before humankind identified and named axons and dendrites. Stone Age babies learned what they needed to know to survive in their environments, Bronze Age babies learned what they needed to make a living in the Bronze Age, and infants in the industrial age thrived then. Admittedly, infant mortalities were high and life was brutish, but enough infants and toddlers from each of those ages grew to adulthood with the knowledge, imagination, skills, and drive needed to advance human civilization.

The human brain's neuroplasticity—its ability to change with experience or after injury—makes it a very flexible and adaptable structure and is one of the reasons humankind has been able to adapt so successfully to new challenges. Baby brains want to learn, they want to know, they want to engage their environments, they want to have physical contact with the physical world they encounter, they want to socialize, they want to develop relationships, they want to classify what they encounter, and they want to understand how it all works.

What our growing knowledge of the internal functioning of infant and toddler brains *has not* revealed is how to make super babies. We cannot fill infant A with information B when developmental window C is open and end up with a great mathematician or expose toddler X to stimuli Y when the brain is primed to learn Z and end up with an inspiring poet. The sad reality is that there are factions in our society pushing super-baby agendas. We will look closer at these agendas and their impact in the next chapter. For now, be aware that a world like the

one created by Garrison Keillor in his stories of Lake Wobegon, "where all the children are above average," is not our reality.

What the growing knowledge of infant and toddler brains *has* revealed is that what responsive, thoughtful, and intentional caregivers do naturally just happens to be what young children really need to make the most of brains that want to think and learn. Imagine that—babies are born ready to learn, and we are instinctively ready to give them what they need to best facilitate that learning. The problem here is that we often fail to listen to our instincts, we ignore our inner voices, and we second-guess ourselves.

. . . .

TAKING CARE OF THE CHILDREN

Identifying Quality Care

Identifying quality infant and toddler care can be tough. Here are some benchmarks to look for when evaluating your own program or when selecting a caregiver.

Goodness of fit: The most important requirement in a child care setting is a good fit between the caregiver and the child. The second most important requirement is a good fit between the parents and the caregiver. These relationships are what healthy emotional environments are built on, and if they are not solid, the caregiving arrangement is not going to work.

Adult-to-child ratio: The fewer children an adult cares for the better. In the United States, 1:4 is the average ratio for children under the age of two. Adults caring for too many children tend to be more stressed, and it is more difficult for them to respond to all the needs of the children in care. Programs with good adult-to-child ratios are more apt to have healthy emotional environments.

Small group size: Young children do better in small group settings. Large groups are overwhelming, and quiet children can become lost in all the noise and activity of a large group. Small groups make it easier for lasting emotional relationships to form.

Continuity of care: Strong emotional environments take time to form, so it is better for children to have the same caregiver for extended periods. Ideally, a child would have the same caregiver for the first three or four years of life. This continuity of care builds strong connections between the caregiver and the child and between the caregiver and the child's family.

Bendy Brains

Brenden, the one-year-old I mentioned in the introduction who is always in four-wheel drive, does not believe in gravity yet. Instead of stepping down when he approaches a step or incline, he keeps walking as if there were no change in topography. Watching him walk down stairs is like watching Wile E. Coyote chase the Road Runner off a cliff. He walks straight out into midair, stands there for a few seconds, looks down, and crashes to the surface below. He does this over and over again, just like Wile E. I half expect him to pull a little wooden sign from nowhere as he begins his fall that says "HELP!" just like in the cartoons.

Despite all the falling he's done since he first started pulling himself up and cruising around, he has not been hurt. He gets a bruise now and then and has bitten his lip a few times, but his four-wheel-drive baby body is flexible and resilient. The human body is made to fall down a lot when it is young. Infants and toddlers come equipped with bendy bones, flexible joints, and a low-to-the-ground design that helps compensate for their clumsiness and inexperience while navigating the world.

The human brain is bendy too. If we make an effort to be responsive, thoughtful, and intentional caregivers, their supple little minds will respond. The brain is born ready to respond to the environments it encounters and the stimulation it experiences. The human mind's inborn flexibility means we do not have to be perfect caregivers and parents. This neuroplasticity makes Brenden's bendy brain as flexible and ready to take on its environment as his bendy body. His brain is busy making connections that will help him eventually figure out gravity and many other wonderful things as he plays, explores, and discovers in the rich environments through which he now stumbles.

The brain's plasticity also holds amazing potential for children born with physical anomalies or into environments lacking the richness of Brenden's. According to the book *Rethinking the Brain* (Shore 1997),

> There is now ample scientific support for the view that the brain is not a static entity, and that a person's capacities are not fixed at birth. The brain itself can be altered—or helped to compensate for problems—with appropriately timed, intensive intervention. . . . The bottom line is that the brain's plasticity presents us with immense opportunities and weighty responsibilities (36–37).

Brains are most bendy and adaptable during the first decade of life, so early recognition of problems is important if they are to be addressed while the brain is most flexible. The "intensive intervention" Shore writes about can range from thoughtful and engaging care environments to surgery and can address issues hindering development, such as epilepsy, vision problems, autism, parental depression, and extreme poverty.

Wile E. Coyote will keep running off that cliff, but soon enough Brenden's brain will make the connections needed to bring his energetic body under control and help him understand gravity. The rest of this book focuses on helping you learn to make the most of those bendy brains with which babies are born.

. . . .

TAKING CARE OF YOURSELF

Which Dog Do You Feed?

> A young girl is camping with her grandfather. They spend the day fishing, hiking, chasing bugs, and watching the wind blow. At the end of the day, they sit by a crackling fire and watch the stars. The grandfather speaks. "I have two dogs that live inside me: a good dog and an evil dog. The evil dog is always fighting the good dog."
>
> His voice fades and he begins poking the fire with a stick.
>
> The girl waits for the rest of the story. She sits patiently for five minutes. After ten minutes, she begins to squirm. In fifteen

minutes, she can barely contain her curiosity. After twenty minutes, she bursts out, "Grandfather, which dog wins?"

The old man turns to look her in the eye and responds, "The one I feed the most." Then he turns his attention back to the fire.

The evil dog wins the inner struggle when allowed to feast off stress, anxiety, tension, fear, hate, frustration, anger, and all the other negative food that seems so readily available. The good dog wins when it feeds on the positive things in life: hope, love, happiness, joy, grace, and all the others. The camping trip with his granddaughter was food for the old man's good dog. The dog that wins the fight determines our outlook and life view.

Feeding the evil dog seems to be the default setting for the human mind. Most of us find it easier to feed our evil dog, since it is so easy to find it food; all you have to do is turn on the television or pick up a newspaper. Feeding your good dog takes effort; you have to actively seek out good food. My good dog feeds daily on the growing independence of my teenage children, my wife's smile, and random interactions with interesting friends and strangers.

Take a moment now and list some of the food your good dog likes to nibble. Keep the list close as a reminder to feed your good dog. Go through your day intentionally, seeking opportunities to feed it the wonder, joy, and hope the world offers.

It Takes Nature and Nurture

I admit to some bias, but if you have ever met my children, you probably agree that they are genetically superior human specimens. Not perfect, mind you, but well above average. You can tell by looking at them that their gene pool is deep and wide. It's not a thin, weak, tepid, soupy pool. I see it more like a hearty salsa, with chunks of fresh heirloom DNA, spicy nucleotide sequences, and tangy microtubules, all mixed in perfect proportion. Other gene pools look over the fence with envy at the gene pool my kids came from and think, "Dang, it sure is green over there! I've got to get off the couch and do something to keep up with the Johnsons."

I could go on, but I won't, because in the end it is not all about genes and heredity. The fact is that the environment they have grown up in has as much to do with my children's greatness as the glorious genetic contributions their mother and I happily made at conception.

I just read the previous two paragraphs to my wife, Tasha, and she suggested that it might be a little much and even proposed that some readers may feel their children's gene pools are as good as or even better than the pools from which our babies sprung. Part of me wants to laugh aloud at such a notion, but I concede that you may not think my children are as near perfect as I do—and I suppose you have every right to your opinion. We will have to agree to disagree about this so that we can move forward.

We may not agree on who has the best genetic code, but I hope we can agree that creating a thriving toddler is a combination of nature and nurture. What children are born with is important, but what they encounter in their early years is vital too. Infants are not born knowing all they need to know to survive and thrive, and they are not born empty vessels that we fill with information. Unlike plankton, earthworms, turkey vultures, and fruit bats, human babies need years of nurturing and care before they are fully able to take on their world. They are born with a desire and drive to know the world, but it takes years of experiences and interactions to acquire the skills needed to leave their nests.

The rest of this chapter and this book look at making the nurture side of the nature-plus-nurture equation as strong as possible for infants and toddlers. It also discusses how our adult choices influence children's learning environments. We'll look at these essential principles of infant and toddler nurturing:

- feed brains and bodies
- care for you to care for them
- take clues from their cues
- get attached
- play every day
- tune in to temperaments

- focus on routines

- seek continuity

- drive learning with interests

- allow self-direction

- let them do it

- build brains with repetition

- devote time to learning

- stimulate, but don't overstimulate

- choose small groups

- love language

Feed Brains and Bodies

Our sedentary lifestyles and an abundance of overly processed foods have led to growing health risks and waistlines. According to Tiffany Sharples's December 6, 2007, article at www.time.com, "Lifelong Effects of Childhood Obesity," there are around nine million overweight children in the United States. Sharples explains that childhood obesity can lead to lifelong health problems. She quotes Dr. Kelly Brownell, director of the Rudd Center for Food Policy and Obesity at Yale: "If you're trying to prevent this problem, then you want to establish good food habits early. You want to keep children away from the food industry messages to eat unhealthy food. It could be that earlier years will be the best time to begin that education."

Teaching healthy eating habits is not as easy as it sounds. Unhealthy fast foods, prepackaged processed foods, and the seemingly ever-present advertisements promoting them, are hard to escape. Our rushed and hectic lives make it challenging to shop for, prepare, and sit down to a healthy meal. Parents and children are bombarded with the message that eating unhealthful food is okay. It takes work to make sure young children eat nutritiously, but here is a sobering statistic from Sharples: by 2020, the annual number of U.S. deaths from heart disease caused by obesity for people thirty-five to fifty years old will increase by 100,000 to 300,000. These are scary numbers.

Parents and caregivers are at the front line in the fight for healthy children, and we have to stand up and do what is right. More agreement exists on the importance of healthy diet and exercise routines than on the impact of weight. We need to teach healthy eating and exercise habits early. We need to avoid overly processed foods: foods high in saturated fats, additives, empty calories, salt, high fructose corn syrup, and other sugars. We need to model these behaviors. It is not enough to talk about them. The toddler sitting across the table from you is more likely to eat her vegetables if she sees you eating yours. She is also more likely to go outside and play if you lead the way to the door. Your day-to-day choices have a huge influence on the children in your care. The next chapter deals with making more mindful choices as you care for and interact with young children.

Care for You to Care for Them
As a caregiver or parent, you take on the role of nurturer. To do the best job at nurturing infants and toddlers, you have to invest regularly in your own care and well-being. Every year, I do dozens of presentations on this topic around the country, and I have heard a lot of stories about stressed caregivers who not only fail at nurturing but put young children in physical danger due to their own stress-related thoughtlessness, inattention, and fuzzy thinking. If you are tired, stressed, on edge, unfocused, run-down, empty, and emotionally frazzled, you are not going to do your best for your young charges. When we fail to take care of our own needs, our patience wears thin, our ability to read and react to children's cues and signals falters, our energy levels decline, our minds wander, and our sense of humor vanishes. A caregiver who is impatient, unresponsive, tired, distracted, and humorless is a poor nurturer and a bad caregiver.

This is a big deal. Every year small children die at the hands of parents and caregivers who are driven to their edge and then one step further. A June 15, 2007, press release from National Association of Child Care Resource and Referral Agencies (NACCRRA) points to ten child deaths in a six-month period in child care programs across the country. That press release called for more state and federal government oversight and regulation. Such oversight and regulation may or may not be needed; no amount of oversight, regulation, or red tape will keep a stressed parent or caregiver from going over the edge.

What does make a difference is individual responsibility. As parents and caregivers, we must be responsible for the choices we make about our own care and the care of children. The one-on-one dance between child and caregiver can't be choreographed from outside. Caregivers who want high-quality, nurturing, thoughtful, and child-centered interactions have to commit to their own self-care. Parents, agencies, organizations, and other entities promoting this type of care must commit to assuring that the adults in any caregiving environment have the resources needed to perform their jobs in a thoughtful and focused manner.

The importance of self-care will be discussed in more detail in chapter 3, and tips and tools for investing in your own well-being will appear throughout the book.

Take Clues from Their Cues

> Sitting in a shaded corner of my yard and reading, I notice a blonde blur zipping toward me at top toddler speed. A moment later Siddha crashes into me, grabs my hand, looks up bright-eyed, and asks, "Tik-kul?"
>
> I work my fingers under her arms to find a ticklish spot, and ask, "Here?"
>
> "No."
>
> I move my hands to the ticklish spot on her tummy. "Here?"
>
> "No."
>
> I find the ticklish spots above her knees. "Here?"
>
> "*Yes!*" she giggles. "Tik-kul!"
>
> She cackles joyfully as I gently tickle the agreed-upon ticklish spot for a few seconds, then nuzzles her head into my side as I rub her back a few times. After a few moments, she is reenergized and zooms off to the sandbox to dig.

Siddha has only recently started using words to communicate what she wants from her environment. *Tik-kul* is one of her first words. This does not mean we have not been communicating for a very long time. Tasha and

I have been caring for Siddha in our family child care program since she was a few months old, and we have worked hard to read and respond appropriately to the cues and signals she uses to let us know what she needs. Her new words just deepen our ability to communicate and respond to each other, making our exchanges more accurate. When she was smaller, we relied much more on her body language and tone to understand what she was trying to communicate. This system worked most of the time because of our close bond, but it was not foolproof. There were times when the only thing we could read in her face was her frustration with our inability to give her what she needed.

Effectively reading and responding to the signals infants and toddlers send is an important part of parenting and caregiving. Giving them what they need when they need it makes the lives of everyone involved easier and happier. When we are unresponsive or unreceptive to their cues, we severely reduce the quality of our interactions and their quality of care. In their book *Einstein Never Used Flash Cards* (2003), authors Kathy Hirsh-Pasek, Roberta Michnick Golinkoff, and Diane Eyer write, "Getting baby off to a good start in the social realm is easy and requires no special classes or videos. Interaction is key—and a lot of it. It's important, however, that this interaction be responsive; it needs to follow the baby's cues" (186).

We will look more at the importance of responding to children's cues in chapters 3 and 4.

Get Attached

Responding regularly and reliably to their cues and signals helps babies and their caregivers form strong and lasting attachments. Two key ingredients in building these bonds are time and predictability. Babies form attachments to adults they see on a regular basis who become predictable parts of their lives. Previously it was believed that the attachment figure had to be the mother, but Hirsh-Pasek and Golinkoff report that research now shows babies attach "not to a single person but to a network of people" (188–89). From early in life, babies work to build emotional connections with a number of people. These early attachments give infants and toddlers a strong footing and help them adjust during their early years.

The drive to form these attachments is strong in infants. They are biologically ready to build relationships from birth. In the 1950s, Professor Harry Harlow of the University of Wisconsin experimented to see if young monkeys were more interested in a hardwire mesh "mother" who offered food or a cuddly terry cloth "mother" without food. The young monkeys opted overwhelmingly for the cuddly surrogate mommy (Harlow 1958).

Speaking of mommies, one of the hardest things I have had to get used to as a male child care provider is toddlers calling me mommy when they start using words. It took some time to get used to having small children periodically run across the room to me with outstretched arms and a gleeful "Mommy!" This has also raised the eyebrows of a few mommies over the years. We can blame this on toddlers' limited vocabularies—anyone who is around to meet their needs and care for them becomes a mommy, just like any animal with four legs becomes a kitty or puppy. They never call me mommy for long. Soon they learn to say "Je" or "Eff."

The significance of attachments is an important theme throughout the rest of this book because it is such a central component of quality infant and toddler care.

Play Every Day

Infants and toddlers have a biological drive to explore and discover the world through play. Play is the tool the brain uses to collect and filter the vast amount of information needed to make those trillions of neural connections discussed earlier in this chapter. It has been said that play is the work of children and that they take their work very seriously—although it may not look so serious to a casual observer. When we look closely at their play, however, we see that they are working hard to understand and control their quickly growing and changing bodies, discover and master new skills, classify and make sense of the world they encounter, and know their feelings and emotions.

Play is deep and important work that looks deceptively simple on its surface. When most people look at playing babies, they only see that surface—wiggling and mouthing their own toes, tightly grasping fragile spring flowers handed to them by older children, twisting and squirming on their back until they surprise themselves and flip onto their tummies, repeatedly (and joyfully) dropping spoons from high chairs, sitting on hands and knees, panting like puppies until they are patted on the head, taking tentative first steps, dropping plastic dinosaurs in the toilet, and scribbling with crayons on the living room wall. These are all images of children hard at play.

The problem is that we adults often misinterpret what we are seeing when young children go about their work. Repeatedly dropping things from their high chairs, playing in the toilet, and writing on the wall get babies in trouble when we should really be giving them more opportunities to discover gravity, play in the water, and color.

Another problem is that adults impose themselves on the play of children. Whole industries have grown up over the past few decades around the mistaken belief that they can improve upon a child's natural inclination to play by offering them gizmos and gadgets. Other well-intentioned but misguided grown-ups seem to think our babies should forget about their childish inclination to play and get serious about learning at earlier and earlier ages. The problem here is that stealing play from babies hurts their development and takes the fun out of childhood.

In chapter 2, we will look more at adult efforts to control or take away play, and in chapter 4, we will delve deeper into promoting child-centered and age-appropriate learning through play, exploration, and discovery.

Tune In to Temperaments

A person's temperament is the way he or she responds to the world. Some toddlers—like Brenden—are four-wheel-drive babies, eager to take on the world at full speed. Others are more tentative, less likely to rush headfirst into new situations, slower to warm to new people and stimuli. I have known many such children over the years. When my son, Tyler, was small, he would not venture off a blanket in the yard because he did not like the feel of grass on his bare feet. His mother also tunes in to her environment—disorder and messes put her off.

Knowing a child's temperament—and your own—is important. There could be stress and conflict if the way you respond to the world is vastly different from the way a baby you care for responds to his. Understanding differences in temperament makes tuning in to children and understanding their needs much easier. Knowing their temperament will help you better understand and respond to their cues and signals.

Paying attention to temperament will also improve your adult relationships. It took time, but Tasha and I have learned much about each other's way of interacting and responding to the world, and this knowledge has made it easier for us to live together. We are more in tune. Over the years, we have both lost some of our rigidity. I'm a natural slob, but I try to pick up after myself more to make her happy. She prefers a lot of planning but over the years has become more spontaneous and less cautious about trying new things.

Understanding temperament can make you not only a better parent or caregiver but a better spouse. We will look more at temperament in chapter 3.

Focus on Routines

Infants and toddlers are creatures of habit; their lives flow better when the day unfolds predictably. At our house, lunch is always followed by hand washing, diaper changing or pottying (with more hand washing), story time, and then naps. What's more, every day everyone sits in the same chair, we follow the same procedures for getting food to the table and clearing the table, we sit in the same place when we read, and we follow regular naptime rituals. I have to tell you, the sameness of it drives me a bit batty sometimes. Occasionally I wish a purple elk with green pinstripes would walk through the dining room just to mix things up a bit. A little surprise now and then would liven up my day—having crazy characters from a Dr. Seuss book stop by to play right when we were sitting down to read *Brown Bear, Brown Bear, What Do You See?* (again) would be a blessing. We'd skip naptime, make a huge mess, and clean it up just before the first parent walked in at the end of the day. It would be such a fun and exciting adventure!

Unfortunately, the world and our caregiving schedule do not revolve around me. The children in our care relish routine, prefer predictability, and smile at sameness. Life is so fresh to them, and they are working so hard to understand all that is going on, that routines act as anchors. Remember how Siddha needs a good "tik-kul" sometimes? The other day she came to me with her request while I was in the kitchen. I bent down to play the tik-kul game right then and there with her, but she just stared at me with a confused look. Then she took me by the hand, walked me to the playroom, and had me sit where I usually am sitting when we play this game inside. Siddha, and all infants and toddlers, are creatures of habit.

We will take a closer look at using routines to promote strong emotional environments in chapter 3 and as a way to enhance play, exploration, and discovery in chapter 4.

Seek Continuity

Small children thrive with regular routines and schedules, but continuity of care is also important. Having the same one or two caregivers day after day, ideally for the children's first few years of life, is a huge benefit for them. This continuity allows the formation of deep and long-lasting bonds between children and their caregivers.

I worked in center-based child care settings for sixteen years before moving to family child care. In my experience, one of the biggest advantages to family-based programs is the continuity of care during the early years of life. In way too many centers, children move from one room to another with nearly every birthday, or even more often. The thing I have enjoyed most about family-based child care is the opportunity we have to see children grow from year to year. This stability allows us to really know the children and understand what makes them tick. It allows us to understand their temperaments, their learning styles, their interests, and their unique personalities.

We will look more closely at the impact of continuity of care when we discuss emotional environments in chapter 3.

Drive Learning with Interests

From very early on, children's interests drive their learning. Children are born with biologically ingrained curiosity: they are interested in what makes the world tick. A child's interest may be fleeting or long lived, or may even end up lasting a lifetime. Hold up a never-before-seen object to a five-month-old, and in all likelihood she will reach out to grasp it, manipulate it, mouth it, and drop it when she grows bored. Older infants will spend longer than expected periods of time fiddling with interesting items. Toddlers become possessive; their items of interest often become "Mine!" They form strong attachments to objects that hold importance and meaning. Older toddlers become interested in cars, dinosaurs, books, music, junk food, painting, writing, cartoon characters, video games, numbers, building, and many other topics—and carry that interest with them throughout childhood and into adulthood.

As you can see from the list above, young children are not always interested in things that are good for them. As parents and caregivers, we must be aware of how our actions are influencing the interests of the children in our lives. They are always watching us and learning from what they see. If a toddler sees her primary caregiver sitting on the couch for hours playing violent video games, swilling grape soda by the gallon, and gulping powdered donuts, what interests do you think that child will develop?

Children will often develop interests worlds apart from those of their caregiver, but we must always remember that they are watching and that our actions speak volumes. Adults responsible for the care and well-being of young children are *professional role models*. We may not always like that job title, but we are stuck with it. We can use their naturally occurring interests (and our influence) to drive learning through play, exploration, and discovery of the world.

We will look more at being professional role models and at how we influence children's interests in chapter 2. In chapter 4, we will look at how to best use their interests to support learning.

Allow Self-Direction

Since infants and toddlers are biologically ready at birth to learn through play, exploration, and discovery, it is no big surprise that they prefer those activities to be self-directed. While we can guide them in the direction of certain toys and activities, we always have to remember that they are the deciders. They will decide what interests them and how they want to act on those interests.

We obviously cannot allow infants and toddlers to direct their entire schedule—chaos would ensue. We adults would spend entire days repeatedly bending over and picking up brightly colored plastic keys. We would sing "Little Bunny Foo Foo" for hours on end. We would have to eat those little jars of turkey dinner. Aside from the way they would torture us, we can't let them run the show all the time, because they are just babies and really don't know anything about the way the world works. Do you think babies know where clean diapers even come from?

Sadly, many families allow children under the age of three to control the household. Families allow babies to decide who sleeps when and where, what goes in the cart at the grocery store, and many other important things better left to responsible adults. As the adults, we have to be in control, but we have to allow them opportunities to self-direct and make choices about how they engage the world. In our family child care program, we work very hard to create physical environments that are safe, healthy, and engaging. We assure that the setting is clean, that the electrical outlets have covers, that there are no choking hazards, and dozens of other things before a child enters the playroom. We also make a variety of stimulating and interesting materials available for play, exploration, and discovery. We do these things behind the scenes, in the background. Once the environment is set, we relinquish much of our control and allow the children to choose what they play with and how they play. We have control over the setting but allow them to control how they interact with that setting, stepping in as needed to provide guidance and assistance. We also have to refrain from programming every second of every day with activities *we* think they need. Small children are experts in determining their own learning needs and filling their time to meet those needs.

In the next chapter, we will look at how some little babies and toddlers end up being their household's deciders (and how you can retain the job of decider for yourself). In chapter 4, we will look at how self-direction fits into the promotion of learning through play, exploration, and discovery.

Let Them Do It

As soon as infants and toddlers can do something for themselves, they want to do it for themselves. In our family child care program, toddlers start carrying their own sippy cups to the table at mealtime as soon as they are steady walkers (part of the sacred lunchtime routine I mentioned earlier). They also help pick up toys, pull up their pants after a diaper change, and put on their own shoes as soon as they seem ready for those tasks. Letting small children do for themselves helps solidify their skills, makes them feel powerful, and develops their sense of self. It also can become frustrating to the adults involved for a number of reasons.

First, it's hard to see them grow up. Let's face it: they are really cute when they are little and they don't stay that way very long. It is very difficult for caregivers and parents to accept that the baby is not a baby anymore. Many of us adults keep doing things for small children as a way of keeping them little. The second reason we often have a hard time with the younglings doing for themselves is that we like to feel needed and we like to take care of them. It makes us feel good and important to have them depend on us. Letting them do things for themselves makes us feel less useful. Third, letting them do things for themselves can be very time consuming and annoying. 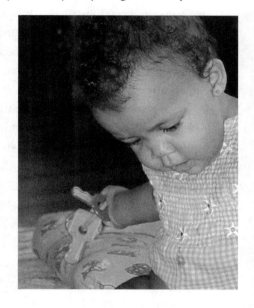 Since they are inexperienced and still developing muscle control, simple tasks like taking off their shoes or bringing their plate from the table to the kitchen counter can take much longer than it would for an adult to do the same thing. It is also very annoying to watch a well-intentioned toddler make a huge mess while trying to help.

This innate drive for independence is quelled in some cultures that prefer prolonged dependence. There is nothing wrong with this. Children grow to adulthood healthy and happy with a variety of child-rearing theories and cultural practices. My preference is early emotional interdependence, which leads to independence at a child-directed pace.

I believe letting children do for themselves is best for their development but not necessarily easy for us adults. We must be thoughtful and focused. We must make sure we make good choices instead of easy choices.

We will look more at dealing with the difficulties of choosing right over easy in chapter 2 and at providing opportunities for children to do things for themselves in chapter 3.

Build Brains with Repetition

Infants and toddlers learn through repetition. Those all-important connections between neurons survive to adulthood when they are repeatedly used. This is why young children love to sing the same songs, read the same stories, do the same puzzles, build the same block towers, and play the same games over and over and over and over and over and over and over again.

With repetition, children gain understanding. Dropping those brightly colored plastic keys again and again teaches that the keys will *always* fall down. They will never fall up. They will never fall sideways. They will never hover in midair. They will *always* fall down. Small children need to prove things we take for granted. They need to experiment and make sure their theories are correct. They need repetition.

The same repetition that literally helps build their brains into efficient thinking machines can drive us adults up a wall. We get it—the keys always fall *down*, blocks always make a loud crash when they hit the floor, the puppy still does not like to have his tail yanked, Mommy doesn't want the laundry *un*folded, little things found on the floor never go in your mouth, and in the book, Silly Sally always makes it to town even though she was sleeping backwards upside down a few pages ago. We get it, but they don't. They need the repetition, and we need to support their need without driving ourselves batty.

We will spend more time with repetition in chapters 3 and 4. We will spend more time with repetition in chapters 3 and 4. We will spend more time with repetition in chapters 3 and 4. We will spend more time with repetition in chapters 3 and 4. (Did you learn where we are going to discuss repetition from all that repetition?)

Devote Time to Learning

Young children learn with amazing quickness and agility, but all that repetition takes time. One of the important things we adults can do to help promote learning for infants and toddlers is to provide them with blocks of uninterrupted time to play, explore, and discover the world. During these blocks of time, allow them to engage in activities of their own choosing at their own pace. Providing these blocks of time in combination with the things mentioned above will create rich opportunities for new learning and understanding—opportunities for those moments when we see that flash in their eyes that comes with new understanding.

The length of time infants and toddlers will engage in activities of their choosing when they have the leisure to do so amazes me. All it takes is a relaxing spring morning: infants are mesmerized by dust particles dancing in a beam of sunshine, toddlers practice walking up and down the steps without assistance, and nearly three-year-olds hunt for "dangerous bugs" in the yard.

While infants and toddlers need blocks of unhurried, relaxing, stress-free time to know the world, we adults have a difficult time allowing that time. We tend to impose our hurried adult lives on the children sharing those lives. We forget how to sit back and examine sunbeams, we take step climbing for granted, and "dangerous bugs" no longer fascinate us. We even go so far as to expect even very young children to be learning something instead of wasting time playing.

In chapter 2, we look at the choices we make involving time in the lives of infants and toddlers. In chapter 3, we will examine time's role in building strong emotional environments. Time will be a topic of discussion in chapter 4, where we look at learning and language development.

Stimulate, but Don't Overstimulate

By now, it should be obvious that those busy little brains need stimulation to build those all-important neural pathways that form the brain's electrochemical wiring. Too much stimulation, like too much chocolate cake, cold beer, prune pudding, or sunshine, is not good. We want to stimulate the brains of infants and toddlers but not overstimulate them.

Infants will actually turn away from the stimulation or go to sleep if it becomes too much. Toddlers may do the same, or they may just feed on it until they turn into hyped-up little gremlins instead of cuddly little critters like that lovable Mogwai named Gizmo in the movie *Gremlins*. That's right, overstimulating a toddler is like letting Gizmo take a shower while eating a large pizza under a high-pressure sodium vapor lamp at quarter past midnight. Bad things will happen.

The problem here is that overstimulation is one of the foundations on which U.S. society is based. We are all about bigger, brighter, faster, louder, and more, more, more. This is not good for adults, and it is certainly not good for small children.

In chapter 2, we will look at how to make choices that avoid overstimulation; we will touch on this topic in chapters 3 and 4 as well.

Choose Small Groups

We live in a world where bigger is best: bigger cars, bigger houses, bigger portions at restaurants, bigger televisions. We want things bigger, bigger, and bigger. When it comes to group size for the care of young children, however, bigger is not better. When the number of infants or toddlers one caregiver is responsible for gets too big, the quality of care declines. Even with adequate adult supervision, a large group of infants and toddlers in a single room negatively influences quality. Our babies need enough attention from their caregiver and sufficient space to go about the work of play.

In my experience, small groups lead to stronger bonds, not only between the caregiver and children, but also among the children. These groups are familial, intimate, and secure, leading to deeper relationships and more learning.

Small groups make caregiving easier on adults and children. We will look more at group size in chapters 3 and 4.

Love Language

Those busy little brains come to us biologically ready to acquire language and are listening for it even before birth. They are primed to learn the language(s) they interact with most during their earliest years. One of the best things we can do to help infants and toddlers learn is to assure that they are surrounded by real, everyday, run-of-the-mill, conversational language. Language is power—it not only allows them to communicate with others, but it also allows them eventually to learn in ways other than direct experience.

Think about it: before we had written or spoken language, the only way to know there were giant saber-toothed tigers roaming the area was to have some direct contact with a giant saber-toothed tiger. After spoken language developed, one group of wandering nomads could tell another group of wandering nomads, "Don't go that way, there are giant saber-toothed tigers over there," and once written language came along, "Beware of Giant Saber-Toothed Tigers" signs could be posted in appropriate places. (It was shortly after this that someone posted the first sign pointing to Wall Drug in Wall, South Dakota.) Language is important because it helps us know things without having experienced them (among other reasons). I don't know about you, but I am a lot more relaxed and comfortable knowing that someone can use language to inform me that giant saber-toothed tigers are migrating through my neighborhood.

Language also helps us communicate ideas and images to others: giant purple saber-toothed tiger on roller skates wearing an Elvis jumpsuit and licking a chocolate ice-cream cone. What are you thinking of right now? See how powerful language is?

There are many ways to use the power of language. In chapter 2, we will look at how language influences the choices we make in relation to infants and toddlers. Chapters 3 and 4 will address language development as well.

. . . .
TAKING CARE OF YOURSELF

Trusting Your Gut

You know that little voice you hear inside your head? The one telling you that you should eat healthier, exercise more, and get a few hours more sleep every week, the one that is always pushing you to do the right thing even when the right thing is the hard thing, the one that sometimes sounds too much like your mother or father or some other adult from your youth who always pushed you to make the right choice? Well, you need to get in the habit of listening to that voice when it comes to infant and toddler care.

Our busy lives and all the attendant stress and mental clutter make it hard to hear that voice sometimes. It gets very weak or sounds like it is coming to us from a long way off, but we have to hone our skills for hearing and responding to it. You can call this voice whatever you like: gut, conscience, soul, intuition, instinct. What matters is that you learn to tune in to it and trust what it is telling you. Whether you are making a choice about how you raise your children, whom you entrust with the care of your baby, or how you go about caring for someone else's child, your inner voice is generally a reliable guide. Listening to it is a good way to start the process of making a mindful decision. The meditation techniques shared throughout this book are a great way to tune in to your inner voice and learn to trust it.

Trusting your own judgment has another benefit: the young children in your life will observe your decision-making methods and learn to trust their inner voices as well. For your well-being and theirs, the next time you find yourself second- or triple-guessing a decision, pause for a moment and listen to what your inner voice has to say.

As I sit writing this, my son, Tyler, is three days away from his seventeenth birthday. In my family, we are long past those years of infant and toddlerhood. The speed at which he learned and grew leaves me speechless sometimes. I will always carry an image of him a few days old in his mother's arms, so content, so tiny, so perfect.

Fast-forward seventeen years. I mean *fast*-forward. In the blink of an eye, that little baby has grown to stand around six feet tall and has feet the size of a few small European nations. He has a deep voice and easy manner. He has great people skills and makes friends quickly. I look at him with pride, because somehow we have raised that tiny baby into a young man who is much politer, kinder, and more thoughtful, confident, and self-assured than I was at his age.

On the one hand, Tasha and I lucked out—he has been an easy child to care for. His temperament and personality balanced easily (for the most part) with ours. He's just been easy to parent. On the other hand, we like to think we have made some choices in his upbringing that helped him grow into the wonderful person he has become.

In the end, there is no one right way to raise a child. There are many ways to do it right. In fact, their bendy brains are so resilient and primed for learning that we can even make a mistake now and then. We do not have to be perfect caregivers or parents to raise happy and healthy children. Over the years, I have interacted with children from vastly different cultures, socioeconomic backgrounds, and family structures. One thing these children reared in vastly different settings have in common is that they are happy and normal kids. Babies are born wired for success. That makes it easier for us adults to get it right than to get it wrong. If you trust your gut and do what you think is right in any given moment, chances are you'll get it right. Although so much depends on chance and circumstance, getting it right also depends a great deal on the choices made by parents and caregivers. In the next chapter, we will look at how adult choices affect what we know about early learning's impact on the lives of infants and toddlers.

Chapter 2

Making Mindful Choices for Infants and Toddlers

Tyler was such an easy baby and brought so much joy to our lives that Tasha decided we needed another one when he was about a year old. I thought it was a great idea. A few days later, she was pregnant. Nine months later, Zoë poked her head into the world. The most vivid memory I have of that day is seeing Zoë nestled on Tasha's chest a few minutes after her delivery. All I have to do is close my eyes to see the two of them—their faces serene and their breathing synchronized—quick but calm. They worked hard to get to that peaceful moment. Zoë fidgeted a bit from time to time, but Tasha's hand on the back of her head was enough to calm her. She nuzzled and nursed a bit. Streaks of blood and goo from the birthing process marked the crisp white sheets. I remember wanting so much to get my hands on that baby and cuddle her to my chest, but I did not want to ruin this idyllic moment between mother and baby. I kissed them both and drank in the moment, waiting my turn.

Our experience with Tyler left Tasha and me feeling more prepared and confident to meet the challenges Zoë had in store for us, but the warm, fuzzy feelings of meeting your child for the first time can quickly give way to fear, dread, and anxiety when you look too closely at the realities of the world. Many parents and caregivers find the lighthearted joy of a new child swiftly replaced by a looming angst. Newborns with medical issues; the emotional, financial, physical, and physiological challenges that can come with a new child; hormones; and the overwhelming fear that encircles some new parents are all things that can quickly turn joy to angst. This angst taints their worldview and affects their decision making.

In some ways, these feelings are warranted. There are plenty of real reasons to feel angst over the future when we look at the recent past. We have been fighting personal and institutional sexism and racism for generations, a war on drugs for over thirty-five years, and gangs for decades. Too many men are happy to be part of the fun accompanying conception but run from the responsibility of fatherhood. Today's infants and toddlers were born post Bill and Monica, post *Girls Gone Wild*, post 9/11, post Mission Accomplished, post No Child Left Behind, post YouTube, post Katrina, and post Subprime Mortgage Calamity. They have been born into a world of terrorist attacks, political debacles, economic uncertainties, and ethical ambiguities. We live in a world where it seems things start at the bottom and work their way down.

On top of all our self-generated angst, outsiders are trying to add to those feelings for their own personal, financial, or political gain. They play on anxieties, worries, fears, frustrations, and emotional weak spots to sell their ideas, policies, and products. The guilt-ridden pressure they apply to manipulate other people's thinking to their advantage is real and weighs heavily on the shoulders of many parents and caregivers. It takes initiative and energy to see through their self-serving spin and slick pitches.

If we look for them, we will find plenty of things to worry about without much searching. There are bad things happening in the world—valid reasons for angst. The bright side—if we can call it a bright side—is that bad things have *always* been going on in the world. Every generation of children ever to walk the earth was born into a world with problems. Wars, civil unrest, political turmoil, natural disasters, changing social structures, economic struggles, and all the rest are just a part of human existence.

Parents and caregivers want the best for babies and toddlers, but we fear the worst. The best choice in any given situation is often unclear, forcing us into decisions that are hurried or that leave us second-guessing ourselves. Sometimes we are so rushed by life that we hardly have time to think about the choices we are making, and other times we fret, fuss, and fidget over decisions until it feels as if our brains are bleeding.

The ability to make thoughtful choices is an important part of caring for young children. Too many people have a hard time maintaining that ability through the hustle and hum of life. Adults want to do right by young children but have a hard time actually taking the time to think about what right looks like. Angst clouds long-range thinking and blurs insight. What caregivers and parents really need are opportunities for clarity, mindful decision making, and making peace with all the ambiguities. We need to step back and look clearly at the big picture in front of us and make good big-picture choices. Here are some questions to ask yourself when making the right big-picture decision for your life and the children you share it with:

- Is this a good long-term choice for the child?
- Does this choice address a need or a want?
- What outside forces are influencing this choice?
- Will this choice make life easier or more complicated?
- Does this choice really improve life quality?
- Is the result worth the effort?

Investing time in answering these questions when making your personal big-picture decisions will refine your thinking and lead to choices that are more thoughtful and aligned with your worldview. This is important, because as you will see in the next section, outsiders are working hard to sway your thinking and influence your decisions.

TAKING CARE OF YOURSELF

Investing in Self-Care

Doing right by infants and toddlers requires clearheaded thoughtfulness and the ability to be in the moment with them so that we are tuned in to their needs and learning cues. It is challenging to be thoughtful and in the moment consistently over the long term. Most caregivers are so busy taking care of the people around them that they fail to take care of their own needs. They feel there is not time for self-care, or if they have the time, they often feel guilty and selfish about spending time on themselves when everyone else is waiting for his or her piece of attention. Many caregivers also fail at making time for self-care because they do not feel worthy of the time and effort.

Because of these things, getting to the point where we are able to invest time and energy in our own care often requires a shift in thinking. Both parents and caregivers need to look at self-care as an investment. When you invest time and energy in your own care, you will be better prepared to make mindful choices when challenging situations present themselves. You will also be better at tuning in to the needs of the children in your care. When your mind is clear, well-rested, focused, clutter-free, open to new situations, and feeling light, you will deal with people and situations more effectively. You will also have more energy to invest in the things you need to accomplish.

Investing in your own care on a daily basis is the single most important thing you can do to improve the care you are providing to the children and adults in your life. You are worthy of this investment. Making such an investment is not a selfish act: it is an act of thoughtful love and consideration for those around you. When you shift your thinking and look at self-care as an investment, the guilt will slip away and the time will magically appear.

For those of you who need permission to take care of yourself, it's okay to make time to do something you enjoy:

- Go for coffee Saturday morning with a friend.
- Read the Sunday paper in bed with your sweetie.
- Have your nails done or your hair colored.
- Take an aikido or yoga class a few times a week.
- Go for a long walk alone on a sunny afternoon.

Big-Picture World of Marketing

In our media-filled world, marketing and sales messages make it especially difficult for caregivers and parents to make good decisions. In order to resist marketing messages and make our own choices, we need to know a little bit about how marketing works. The sections below on marketing practices, terms, and common persuasion techniques will help you decode those messages and think critically when someone is trying to sell you something that you absolutely have to have in order to care for your babies. The following definitions of marketing and pop culture terms reflect ongoing efforts by marketers and trendsetters to influence your interactions with young children and the ways you spend your money. Knowing these terms will help you better understand their efforts. These are terms I have encountered in conversations with parents and caregivers, on the Internet, and in books, such as Susan Gregory Thomas's *Buy, Buy Baby* (2007) and Susan Linn's *Consuming Kids* (2004).

Terms Specific to Children and Families

Comfort-food property: Brands that soothe and reassure parents and caregivers are called *comfort-food properties.* In her book *Buy, Buy Baby*, Susan Gregory Thomas explains that many of today's moms grew up with Strawberry Shortcake in the 1980s and see the brand as a comfort-food property they can share with their baby girls. American Greetings owns the brand and has released a lot of new merchandise to take advantage of the nostalgia these mommies feel for the brand.

Evergreen property: An evergreen property is a fictional character (that has been around for a long time and is perpetually popular with children and parents) and that has been licensed for merchandising. Evergreen properties generate a lot of income for their owners.

Newstalgia: This term refers to the upgrading, modernizing, and rebranding of toys and characters from the past to create a nostalgic feeling in parents and caregivers. Many evergreen properties are updated periodically to keep them fresh while retaining their nostalgic feeling. This makes the items desirable to both children and their adult caregivers.

Cradle to grave: This is the holy grail for many businesses. They want to achieve cradle-to-grave loyalty from consumers. The goal is to acquire customers when they are as young as possible and keep them buying for life. Evergreen properties tend to possess this kind of loyalty.

Pop Culture Terms

Pester power: This refers to children's ability to whine, nag, and badger adults into making purchases. Marketers encourage pester power because they know it works; they rely on our inability to say no to our children.

Kidfluence: Pester power works because of kidfluence, the direct and indirect influence children have on the purchasing decisions of their parents and other adults. Children used to influence only the kinds of cereal in the pantry. Now they are influencing much larger decisions, such as choices of computers, vehicles, and family vacation destinations.

Coolhunter: A person who hunts for new, up-to-the-minute, cutting-edge trends, styles, and ideas and then sells the information to companies to incorporate into new products. Coolhunters often look to countercultural and fringe ideas and make them mainstream. At first glance, you might think coolhunting applies only to things like popular music and fashion, but coolhunters are also on the lookout for cutting-edge trends in children's clothing, infant equipment, books, and other baby and toddler paraphernalia and trends.

Alpha pup: Alpha pups are the cool kids—even if they are only a few years old. Coolhunters watch playgrounds, parks, shopping centers, parent-child classes, child care centers, and other locales as part of their market research to see what gear, attitudes, and ideas the cool alpha pups and their alpha-dog parents prefer.

Helicopter parent: These are parents who hover over their children, making all the decisions, removing all obstacles, and controlling everything to assure their perfect children live perfect lives—lives free from decision making, failure, missteps, and mistakes. A Black Hawk parent is a Helicopter parent willing to stoop to unethical behavior on behalf of his child (such as buying her way to the top of the waiting list at the "right" child care program).

KGOY: KGOY stands for Kids Getting Older Younger. This is also referred to as *age compression*. This term expresses the idea that children today are supposedly growing maturer and more sophisticated quicker, that they are growing up faster. Young children are aspirational—they want to be like kids slightly older and maturer than they are. They want to have the same possessions and do the same things as the big kids. A certain internationally known blonde doll with big breasts and a tiny waist was popular with eight- to ten-year-old girls a generation ago—now she goes out of favor with many young girls by the age of three or four. Younger children aspired to be like their older siblings and friends, but once this doll made it into the hands of the younger children, the older ones considered it a baby toy and moved on to other things. (Nevertheless, since this doll is an evergreen property and is newstalgic, she is still very popular with older kids and even adults.)

Because of this perception that kids are getting older younger, we often mistakenly expect them to behave and think in ways for which they simply are not developmentally ready. This has meant that younger and younger children are expected to act and learn in developmentally inappropriate ways.

Prostitot: This term refers to young girls who dress and behave as if they are much older and maturer. It's sad that this term exists, but there are a lot of reasons for it. KGOY plays a big part: young girls aspire to dress and act like their big sisters and the women they see in movies and on TV. Marketers create clothing and accessories to feed these aspirational desires. Then parents buy the stuff and allow it to be worn. When I first heard the term years ago, it referred to twelve- to fifteen-year-old girls acting and dressing trampy. Now there is a lot of merchandise readily available for much younger girls that sexualizes them inappropriately. Gum ball machines sell temporary lower back tattoos (known as tramp stamps), and preteen thongs with suggestive sayings can be purchased from many companies. You can even go online and purchase toddler T-shirts and infant onesies with crude sayings I wouldn't want any person to wear, let alone a baby.

Thinking about the sexualizing of babies makes my skin crawl, but if we are going to combat age compression and the sexualizing of young children, we have to be aware of what is going on in the world. If we don't watch out, someone is going to start marketing thong diapers with the phrase "Future Hottie" printed across the front. The sexualization of children is wrong and yet occurs excessively. We need to be offended by it, and we need to act to curb it. If you want to grab a pitchfork and join my mob or read the phrases I could not share here, contact me through my Web site at www.explorationsearlylearning.com.

Common Persuasion Techniques

The constant whizzing and whirring of marketing messages that zip into our ears and bounce off our eyeballs overwhelm most people. Attempts to catch our attention and alter our thinking, to change our choices, and to nudge our noodles in the direction of a particular product, idea, or ideal can crush us. We try to ignore them, we try to make ourselves numb to them, we may even try to hide in the corner of a dark room under a cuddly blanket to get away from them, but those marketing messages are always waiting for their shot at our eyes and ears.

As soon as you take your thumb out of your mouth and pull that cuddly blanket off your head, someone is going to try to convince you to buy something, do something, or think something. We're trapped, and we can't escape; those influential messages are not going to go away. In fact, the persuasion techniques used on us are likely to intensify in their frequency and sophistication—making ignoring, numbing, and hiding even more futile.

So, how do you stand up to the constant onslaught of persuasive marketing messages and make good choices for young children and yourselves? Well, one of the most effective things you can do is understand the tools used to bend your thinking. Knowing these tools helps you take apart the messages you see and hear, making it easier to separate valid arguments from fluff. Identifying and understanding the following tactics when you come across them in your day-to-day life empowers you to make decisions that are more thoughtful.

Appeal to beauty: We are naturally attracted to beautiful people, places, and things. This tactic plays on our desire to be beautiful, live in beautiful surroundings, and have beautiful things.

Celebrity endorsement: This tactic associates products with a well-known person. We are supposed to believe that if we use the product, we will take on the characteristics of the celebrity. When it comes to young children, the celebrity is often a cartoon character specifically designed to appeal to them. This is why animated characters from the movies and TV are so successful at pushing products to children and adults.

Compliment the consumer: Praising consumers who choose their products as good decision makers and thoughtful consumers is another tactic used by advertisers to sell things. They want us to feel smart and good about choosing to do business with them.

Appeal to escape: This tactic appeals to our desire to get away from it all, our desire for adventure, our desire to get away from the humdrum day-to-day responsibilities of our lives. This method sells everything from bubble bath to sport-utility vehicles.

Appeal to independence and individuality: This tactic appeals to our desire to be rebellious and independent thinkers, our desire to chart our own course and live outside the box in which everyone else exists.

Bandwagon/peer approval claims: "Come on, man, try it—everyone is doing it." This tactic uses our desire to fit in and be part of the crowd to sway our decision making. It plays on the same peer pressure that drives middle school fashion and high school drug use. The implied message is "If you're cool, you'll ——."

Appeal to intelligence: Often, people trying to sway our thinking will appeal to our intelligence. They assure us that their product or idea is a smart choice—a choice a thinker would make, a choice someone who can't be deceived would make.

Appeal to lifestyle: This tactic associates products and ideas with particular ways of life and social categories. This technique plays either directly to the lifestyle we have or to a lifestyle to which we aspire.

Nurturing claims: These claims associate products and ideas with our desire to take care of others. They appeal to our parental instincts.

Nostalgic claims: Ah, the good old days. This tactic plays on our fond memories of the good old days. Our longing for the past is so strong that perceptive marketers reposition favorite items and brands from our youth so we will buy them for our children. This has resulted in a lot of baby merchandise with images of characters from Mommy and Daddy's early years. These products tug at our hearts and our fond memories of years gone by.

Fantasy claims: This tactic uses our dreams and fantasies to influence our thinking and decision making. Fantasy is why professional models exist—people dream of either being them or being with them. The Perfect Parent Fantasy sells many products to parents leading average but imperfect lives.

Humorous claims: Laughter forms bonds and lowers defenses, and those bonds and lowered defenses can lead to sales. This is the basis for advertisements featuring talking and dancing babies or bumbling fathers.

Sensory claims: These claims play on our five senses and sell everything from cookies to diapers to family vacations.

Factual/scientific/statistical claims: These claims use science and numbers to convince us to make a specific choice. Just the facts. That is what they want us to believe, but pitches that look like they are using cold hard facts to sell us a product or ideas need a closer look to determine if the scientific and statistical "facts" are actually factual or relevant.

Rhetorical question: This tactic usually asks a question that demands a response affirming the qualities of a product or idea. It is a tool used to bring you into agreement with the marketer's branding of the item they are trying to convince you to buy.

Unfinished claim: These claims slip by when you are not paying attention, but when you stop and look at them, you realize something is missing. "Absorbo is 50 percent more absorbent." More absorbent than what? "Mega-Diapers—better on your baby's bottom!" Better than what?

Weasel word claim: A weasel word modifies and nearly negates the claim that follows. After examining claims using weasel words, you will find they are empty and meaningless. Watch out for these and other weasels: *helps, virtual, acts, works, can be, new, improved, up to, as much as, refreshes, comforts, tackles, fights, the feel of, the look of, fortified, enriched, strengthens.*

"We're different and unique" claim: These claims try to set a product or idea apart from the pack by setting them up as exceptional. We are supposed to believe that the product's exceptional qualities make it superior to its competitors. The uniqueness they are selling us may be something as trivial as the product's color or packaging—remember green ketchup?

"Water is wet" claim: These claims say something about a product that is fundamentally true about any product in the same category. "Wilber's Project Paste is sticky" or "Burt's Baby Bottles hold up to eight ounces." These things are true, but they are also true about their competitor's products. This type of claim obfuscates the truth and confuses our thinking, making it easier to accept other claims that may not be factual.

Marketing messages are still going to be constantly zinging and zooming your way, but knowing these terms should help you deal with them more effectively and allow you to make better choices in what you buy, do, and think. You may still want to hide under that blanket occasionally. That is okay—we all need to be alone from time to time.

. . . .
TAKING CARE OF YOURSELF

Letting Go I

As you begin investing time and energy in your own care, you will probably discover a lot of baggage from past days, weeks, months, and years. When you don't take time for the regular cleaning and decluttering of your own mind, debris builds. In our busy lives, we tend to ignore and suppress the feelings and thoughts we don't think we have time to deal with. We cram these things inside and move on to the next emergency life tosses our way.

People hold on to everything: irritation at people who cut them off in traffic a few hours ago, frustration over life choices made months or years ago, heartaches from youth, self-loathing over perceived failures, fear of changing or not changing, hatred for those who caused physical or emotional pain years or decades ago, and other named and unnamed anger, anxiety, stress, tension, fretfulness, frustration, resentment, hostility, malaise, and melancholy. We carry these things with us—trying to ignore and suppress all of them. When the hard feelings start leaking out, we cram them back inside, hoping they won't show up unexpectedly. As the pile of undealt-with-stuff grows, it becomes harder and harder to contain. Some caregivers have shared with me their decision to wear happy-face masks for the world to cover their inner turmoil.

Carrying this stuff around is a lot of work. Hauling this unresolved emotional luggage wherever you go is both emotionally and physically draining. Besides, even if you think you are effectively hiding it from the world with the best happy-face mask ever devised, infants and toddlers are going to see right through it into your soul.

Take a moment right now and think about all the thoughts and emotions you are carrying around from your past. Really do this—knowing what you are holding on to is the first step to letting it go, and letting go will improve your decision making and focus. It will help you make better choices and tune in to the children you care for more effectively.

As you think of the things you are holding on to, you might be able to let some go as soon as they pop into your head. Just acknowledging these little things is enough to free you from their grasp. Letting go of bigger issues will take more time and effort. Getting a complete list all at once is difficult, so you may need to come back to this task a few times. For now, use the space provided on the page to the right to jot them down. Remember to add to this list later if you recognize additional feelings and thoughts you have suppressed.

Later in the book, we will look at some simple tools to help let go and focus your thinking. The quality of care you provide to infants and toddlers is only as good as the quality of care you provide to yourself.

Hard Choices

The remainder of this chapter focuses on many of the big-picture infant- and toddler-related topics that cause angst for parents and caregivers as well as the interrelated choices they are making about those issues. Parents and caregivers are faced with many concrete choices, such as what diapers to use or how to handle naptime, but they are also faced with more subtle choices they may not even be aware of. For example,

- thinking and intuition versus outside pressure

- right versus easy

- quantity time versus quality time

- less versus more

- face-to-face versus face-to-screen

- living in the moment versus recording the moment

- hope versus fear

- children's needs versus your needs

I chose these topics because they are on my mind a lot as a parent and a caregiver, because they frequently come up in conversations with other parents and caregivers, because I am often frustrated by the lack of thought some people give them, and because the way these issues are addressed affects the emotional environment of any caregiving setting. The choices made about these issues form the foundation of the emotional environment you create.

You can see that I present each of the issues addressed in the list in a *this* versus *that* format. My hope is that drawing a sharp contrast between potential choices will help you think about your thinking on each issue. For example, in the Living in the Moment versus Recording the Moment section, we look at two extremes: fully experiencing moments with children in real time at one extreme and preventing full participation in those moments with a recording device at the other extreme. On one end of the continuum, we are engaged in every moment, and at the other end, we are recording every moment but not participating. Your happy place on this issue is probably somewhere in the middle. Being in the moment is important, but so are those pictures and videos. In this section and all the others that follow, what we are really looking for is balance—a happy choice in the middle that works for you and the children in your care. So, while the section headings present the extremes, I hope you will seek balanced choices. Many right ways exist for thinking about these topics. I hope you will see some nuance in each of them that leads you to the right place for you and for the children you spend time with.

I also hope that you will take time to question some of your current choices. So often we blindly choose products, philosophies, and courses of action without much thought, allowing those powerful outside influences to guide our decision-making process. When you question your own choices now and then, you will find that the ones that work are reinforced and the ones that don't can be changed. You may also find it easier to accept the choices of other people. With this end in mind, each section ends with some questions to help you thoughtfully question your choices. I hope this helps clarify your thinking on these issues and helps you make mindful decisions concerning the children in your care.

Thinking and Intuition versus Outside Pressure

Angst over doing right by infants and toddlers muddies many adults' thinking and makes it difficult to tune in to personal thinking and intuition. It also makes people more susceptible to outside pressure from those looking to play on anxieties, worries, fears, frustrations, and emotional weak spots. As parents and caregivers, we all too often find ourselves unthinkingly making choices that affect young children based on what friends, neighbors, strangers on the Internet, paid celebrity spokespeople, authors, politicians, and commercials suggest instead of relying on our own thinking. These outsiders attempt to influence choices ranging from the brand of diaper we choose to the make and model of car we purchase, from the discipline methods we use to our opinions on play and early learning.

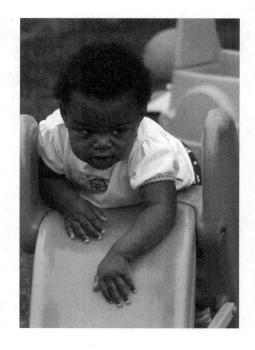

We often lack experience in trusting our own thinking and intuition because we have grown up with others making many of our choices.

- You're three years old, and Grandma asks what you want for snack. You want one of her homemade chocolate chip cookies. Mom says from across the room, "Give her some carrot sticks." Grandma gives you carrot sticks.

- You're eight and hanging out with friends. You want to play tag. They want to sit and watch a movie. You end up watching a movie you have already seen and didn't like.

• You're out to dinner with your sweetheart. After looking at the menu for twenty minutes, you decide on the salmon. The waiter says, "The salmon is dry today; you should have the chicken." You have the chicken. Later, as you are leaving the restaurant, you hear someone raving about how great the salmon was. Meanwhile, your chicken was so rubbery that you dropped a piece and it actually bounced off the floor and hit the waiter in the eye.

The continual implication that our choices are inadequate or ill informed leaves us vulnerable to outside pressure. If the commercials on TV, the family next door, your older sister, and your two-year-old all think you should buy Fruity Colored Sugar Rings, there is a good chance you are going to buy Fruity Colored Sugar Rings.

This influential outside pressure often seeps into our unconsciousness as we go about our lives. While some sources may attempt to sway our thinking concerning infants and toddlers with an in-your-face hard sell, much of the pressure is more understated. For every commercial with a ranting cartoon character trying to sell us Fruity Colored Sugar Rings, there is also an in-law raving about how soft and soothing New and Improved Ultra-Strong Mega-Wipes are on little Waldo's bottom. For every toddler screaming and demanding Frozen Choco-YumYum Treats at the grocery store, there is a print ad showing a happy family quietly rolling down the highway in a new Vista Cruiser Minivan with optional onboard entertainment center. Heck, even this chapter is a quiet attempt to influence you into thinking about the choices you are making concerning infants and toddlers.

These attempts at persuasion are no big deal as long as we are aware of them. Most entities trying to influence our thinking are not malevolent. They might be pushing a cause or trying to make a buck, but they generally mean no one any harm. One of the best strategies for making good choices is to seek opinions from sources we trust. Problems come when we blindly follow without doing any critical thinking. We are making bad choices when we buy Fruity Colored Sugar Rings, New and Improved Ultra-Strong Mega-Wipes, Frozen Choco-YumYum Treats, or Vista Cruiser Minivans based solely on the influence of others. We are making bad choices when we select discipline strategies, cold remedies, or child development theories solely based on the thinking of others. We are making bad choices when we fail to think and to notice how others are influencing that thinking.

The first step to awareness is understanding who is influencing our choices. The outsiders most commonly trying to pressure our thinking include these:

Immediate peer group: Life is a lot like high school: most people feel it is important to fit in with their immediate peer group. As adults, we have a bit more choice about which social group we associate ourselves with, but as in middle school, we often are easily persuaded by the groupthink that emerges from such groups. Your immediate peer group may influence how you dress your baby, what brand of diapers you use, which stroller you purchase, and whether you recycle, among many other choices.

Society at large: We are also influenced by the larger society we operate in on a daily basis. Communities and regions have their own cultures, and those cultures affect our thinking on different subjects. For example, exploratory outside play in a family child care program in West Yellowstone, Montana, looks much different from play in the Lincoln Park neighborhood of Chicago, Illinois.

Government: The actions and inactions of local, state, and national government have a direct impact on the lives of infants and toddlers as well as their parents and caregivers. The ability of these entities to tax and regulate are big influences on parenting and caregiving decisions.

Media/Marketers: Everyone in the world who wants to sell us a product or idea belongs in this group. They want to sway our thinking, earn our loyalty to their brands, and sell us stuff. This is not a bad thing; this is capitalism. It is a powerful force in social and economic development and deserves our respect. Our society relies on these important entities, but we need to be aware of their power and how it influences our decision making.

Infants and toddlers: Somewhere along the line, these tiny little people gained a lot of influence over the decisions of the adults with whom they interact. They have become deciders in diapers. From the time they can point and gurgle out a few words, they are influencing our choices about food, clothing, child-rearing practices, and much more.

The language permeating our lives influences the choices we make about infants and toddlers. Those trying to manipulate our choices rely heavily on language to get the job done. It could be a slick and well-polished multimillion-dollar media campaign, the words "Oh, you're going to buy *that* stroller?" from a friend with an attitude, or a big-eyed "Please, Mommy?" from a two-year-old. In all these cases, language is the primary tool used to influence our choices. These influencers often rely on empathy, vivid imagery, descriptive language, metaphors, and an inclusive tone to sway thinking. The goal is to create strong mental pictures and an emotional response in the audience.

With that in mind, I encourage you to generate your own strong mental pictures and emotional responses when considering how to respond to the outside pressures and the angst they induce. When facing a tough decision, invest time in conjuring up strong word pictures and mental images that will provide a deeper understanding of your own thinking on a topic. These images are helpful in choosing a course of action because you use your prior knowledge, your current frame of mind, and your intuition. These resources often go unused when making choices. This process forces more introspection, consideration, and intention into your decisions. Here are two examples of the process at work.

Years ago, when I was a child care center director, a mother decided to quit a job she loved to stay at home with her young son. She had worked long and hard for her position and loved the corporate world, but she felt jealous of the time the center staff spent with her child while she worked. She spent time visualizing the next few years as a working mom and those same years as a stay-at-home mom. She imagined each option in detail and in the end intentionally chose the option that made the most sense (and lived happily ever after).

I use this process in my own life all the time. I love to take on new projects and try new things, and in the past, this led to stress and burnout. Years ago it got to the point that it nearly killed my marriage. To curb my natural tendency to take on every opportunity that pops up, I now very intentionally create vivid images of my options and let them play out on the inside of my eyelids. The primary goal of this exercise is to make the choice that is best for the maintenance of my relationship with my one true love. The choices are not always easy, but they end up being the right choices.

Turning away from the pull of those outside influences is challenging, but making choices that are really right for you and your situation is freeing and empowering. Here are some questions to ask yourself when considering such decisions:

- Does this choice reflect my values?

- What is the long-term impact of this choice?

- Is this really the right choice?

- What outside sources influenced this choice?

Right versus Easy

One of the best examples of a parent doing the right thing instead of the easy thing I have ever seen happened on a cold fall afternoon. Maddie, almost three, did not want to put on her shoes and socks when it was time to go home from our family child care program. Her mother, Jennifer, tried reasoning, sweet-talking, and the Mommy Voice—none of them got the shoes and socks on Maddie's little feet. Finally, Jennifer stood up and said, "Okay, don't wear your shoes and socks, but your feet are going to get mighty cold walking to the car." Maddie smiled victoriously, and out the door they went. She made it across the porch and down the steps without much problem, but as soon as her little piggies hit the icy cold concrete driveway, her eyes got huge and she wanted to be carried. Jennifer walked to the car. Maddie quickly followed on the tips of her tiptoeing feet. Maddie made a questionable choice and lived with the consequences. She also did a much better job listening to Mommy after that when it was time to put on her shoes. The easy thing would have been to carry Maddie; seeing her baby tip-tip-tiptoeing across the driveway was tough on Mommy but the right choice for Maddie.

When caring for infants and toddlers, parents and other grown-ups have to make a clear choice between what is right and what is easy. Sometimes this boils down to choosing between being the adult and being the buddy.

Over the last forty or fifty years, grown-ups have been more interested in being children's friends or peers than figures of authority. They have become more interested in being liked than listened to, more concerned with being an equal than a role model. This has influenced adult decision making. Many adults are choosing to abdicate their long-term responsibilities for children in favor of short-term companionship. This is generally more observable in interactions between adults and older children, but the groundwork for such dynamics starts in infancy and toddlerhood.

I know a dad who invested a lot of time in being his young son's buddy. They ate stacks of powdered donuts for breakfast every morning, and they stayed up late every night playing violent video games. Dad did everything for his little buddy and gave in to him on most things because he wanted to be liked. Dad was more concerned about short-term popularity than his son's long-term development. This did get him liked, but it also resulted in a child with behavior problems and developmental delays related to the parenting he was receiving.

I have to state emphatically that this guy was a loving and concerned father who wanted the best for his son. They spent a lot of time together and had a strong relationship, but for whatever reason, Dad chose not to step back and see how his desire to be his son's best buddy instead of his father was doing harm.

This is just one small example of being the buddy winning out over being the adult. Busy schedules and broken families have led many adults to try to buy their young children's affection with all types of treats and treasures. To be clear, when referring to "broken families," I am not talking about divorced families or any other family structure. I am talking about families that are in conflict and chaos for whatever reason. Divorce can be terribly hard on children, but so can so-called intact families filled with anger and hatred.

I have talked to caregivers in the Chicago and Los Angeles areas who work in centers where parents pay nearly $400 a week for child care and have full-time nannies for their children. These providers told me that many parents were constantly showering their young children with all kinds of fancy and exotic gifts and indulgences to make up for the time they were unable to spend with them. These loving parents chose being the buddy over being the adult; they chose easy over right.

Who can blame them? Choosing easy is like being Peter Pan or Santa Claus or Batman. Choosing easy means late nights and soda pop; it means ice cream for breakfast five days a week. Easy means saying yes more than saying no. Easy means no limits. Choosing easy means fun and games.

The above examples of choosing easy over right are pretty extreme, and you may not see yourself reflected in them. What about these more common examples: putting off bedtime to avoid the struggle; buying a candy bar from the checkout display to avoid a scene; giving in to random toddler tantrums just to make them stop; giving "one more chance" six or eight times; counting to three using fractions. We all do these things. They *are* easier, but are they *right*? What are we really teaching when we choose easy over right in these everyday situations?

In contrast to choosing easy, choosing right can just plain suck. Choosing right is work. Choosing right does not mean endless days of fun, cotton candy, and rainbows. Choosing right means saying no and sometimes causing tears. Choosing right means setting limits. Choosing right means fruit instead of fruit pies. Choosing right means regular bedtimes. Choosing right means little toes on cold driveways, when the owner of those little toes chooses not to put on her shoes. Our duty is to help children grow into thinking, compassionate, responsible, mature *adults*. Our duty is to choose right.

Since every time we are in the presence of a young child we are looked upon as a role model, it is imperative that we thoughtfully choose right over easy. The problem here is that choosing easy is so—easy. It is easy to let them drink soda. It is easy to feed them fast food. It is easy to give in to their calculated smiles and tantrums. It is easy to let them stay up a little longer. It is easy to become caught up in all the marketing and hype for this product or that. It is easy to believe standing our ground is wrong and going with the crowd is right. It is easy to renounce our responsibility and abdicate our authority. It is easy to choose the easy way out.

Nevertheless, it is not right. It is not right to fill small children with unhealthy food and drink. It is not right to teach them that emotional manipulation is the most effective way to achieve their goals. It is not right to deprive them of much needed sleep. It is not right to buy everything marketers make us think we need. It is not right to teach children to follow blindly, and it is certainly not right to hand over our adult responsibilities and authority to small children.

What's more, when we choose easy over right, we are teaching the children in our care that it is acceptable for them to do the same. This means that choosing easy over right affects young children not only in the short term but for their whole lives. Seeing us make easy choices now will lead them to do so later.

It does not matter if you base your opinions of what is right on your liberal or conservative ideas or your religious or your secular beliefs. What matters is that you make the right choice for your belief system over the quick, expedient, easy choice.

American sociologist Robert King Merton, who taught at Columbia University for most of his career, coined the term *role model*. He believed that individuals compared themselves to "reference groups" of people occupying the social roles to which they themselves aspired. Parents and child care providers are professional role models. Our job is to model consciously and consistently the behaviors we want the children we interact with to emulate. Being the adult in the room means that by default you are the representative of the reference group young children seek to join. They are looking to you as a model while they work to understand the world and gain control of their physical and mental abilities. Simply being the adult that they see means you are the adult they aspire to be. In the end, choosing easy and being the buddy is easier, but it is also the easy way out. Choosing right and being the adult, the professional role model, means acting with more intention, mindfulness, and wisdom. It means that when you say to a group of toddlers, "Pick up the toys, and then we will eat lunch," you do not eat lunch until they have picked up the toys. It means that you follow through when you say, "If you don't quit goofing around and get your coat and boots on, we will go outside without you."

Here are some questions to ask yourself when considering your thinking about right versus easy:

- What would my parents or grandparents have done in this situation?

- What are the long-term ramifications of this choice?

- What am I *really* modeling with this choice?

- How does this choice fit into my belief system?

Quantity Time versus Quality Time

In the end, it is not about quantity time or quality time, because babies need an abundance of both. Infants and toddlers thrive with quantities of quality time. They require scads of attention and all the snuggles, cuddles, and hugs they desire. Sometimes their needs seem to greatly exceed our abilities to meet them.

The problem is that our adult world does not always allow us to provide the quantity of quality that babies crave. Jobs, sometimes multiple jobs, and other obligations keep parents away from their babies longer than they would prefer. While in child care, those same babies may not get the quantity of quality they need because of high caregiver-to-children ratios, high staff turnover, lack of staff training, the demands of other children, and lack of professionalism.

Understand that for small children, true quality time is not short, intense bursts of high activity and attention. This is the kind of quality time some older children receive from guilt-ridden parents on birthdays or during visits with noncustodial parents. This kind of thing should be renamed Rush-Rush-Stressful-Forced-Smiles-Time or Let's-Cram-a-Month-of-Fun-into-an-Hour-Time. This much activity tends to overwhelm and overstimulate infants and toddlers. It is *not* quality time. The kind of quality time infants and toddlers need is quieter and gentler. Time spent chasing runny noses, changing diapers, holding bottles, repeatedly picking up dropped plastic keys, spooning mashed peas into mouths that bob and weave, reading *Brown Bear* repeatedly: this is real infant and toddler quality time. Doing these uncomplicated little things—simply being there for them—is the foundation upon which strong child/caregiver relationships are built. (We will spend more time on the importance of these magically mundane moments in chapter 3.) When we cram a lot of hullabaloo into a little hunk of time, small children are overstimulated and overwhelmed.

Because time is often so limited for parents and caregivers, we feel pressured to force fond memories out of the limited time we can carve from our schedules. This is stressful and rarely manages to meet our inflated expectations. In the end, we often get stuck trying to force too much activity into what we think is too little time. We need to relax and make the most of the time we have, focusing on the simple give-and-take of the relationship. You can get a lot of quality out of a ten-minute walk with a toddler though piles of wet leaves and sidewalk puddles. Ten minutes face-to-face, eye-to-eye, nose-to-nose with an infant is a high-quality way to spend ten minutes. Drastic changes may be required to make quantities of quality time available to the children in your care. Parents may have to think about which priorities to focus on; child care programs may need to consider adding staff or cutting enrollment. Here are some questions to ask yourself while thinking about quantity and quality time:

- How are you investing the twenty-four hours you have each day?

- How would life improve if you had more focused time with the children in your care?

- Are you overwhelmed by your schedule? If so, what can you do about it?

- What can you do to bring more real quality into the time you have with your child?

Less versus More

Comedian George Carlin performed a hilarious bit about all the stuff we have and the need to find a place for it all. I first saw this routine decades ago on the *Tonight Show* with Johnny Carson and remember laughing so hard that my sides ached. The whole routine makes fun of our obsession with accumulating stuff and how to accommodate it all in our busy lives (www.youtube.com/watch?v=MvgN5gCuLac). Carlin was a master with language and at pointing out the absurdities of everyday life.

The way we raise our children is not lacking in absurdity. We are obsessed with our stuff, and this obsession has seeped into the environments in which we care for infants and toddlers. It is amazing to see how much stuff some people require to care for a little baby: baby swing, bouncy seat, high chair, car seat, mobiles, cradle, crib, diaper bag, porta-crib, jogging stroller, strolling stroller, changing table, diaper pails, bottles, burp rags, bundles of disposable diapers, baby wipes, pallets of formula and processed baby food, baby monitors (audio *and* video), digital camera, digital video recorder, prenatal education system, computerized stuffed animals, lapware, infant learning software, toddler learning software, riding toys, DVD player, television, and on and on. On top of that, there are parents with a single child under the age of one driving around in huge SUVs just so they have space to haul all the stuff they need for a one-day outing to Grandma's house.

Not only are we obsessed with baby stuff; it has to be the right stuff. It has to have the right label and be purchased from the right baby boutique or mega-retailer. It has to be what all the other babies in the adult's peer group have—or it has to be *better* than what they have. Adequate is not good enough when extravagant is an option. Following fads has become more important than simple functionality. There is nothing more functional than onesies and sweatpants for infants and young toddlers or T-shirts and jeans for older toddlers. They are simple, easy to get on and off for diaper changes, inexpensive, and durable. Yet we prefer to dress young children like little adults. Why do children under the age of two need pockets? Why do their little overalls have hammer loops and a pocket for pliers? Shoes for infants in the $30–$40 price range are common, and it is easy to find toddler shoes for over $70. Do little feet that can't even walk yet need such expensive shoes that they will quickly outgrow? Why do we put them in shoes that make mastering the complicated process of walking difficult if not downright dangerous? Why do we put slippery tights and leggings on baby girls who are learning to crawl? Why do little girls who are learning to stretch, bend, climb,  run, and jump get stuck in dresses and warned to keep their hems down and knees together? Why do stuffed animals need to talk, shake, and try to teach? Why do toddlers need televisions and DVD players in their bedrooms? Why do we stick our infants in swinging, bouncing, swiveling, vibrating, giggling, and whirring contraptions that overstimulate them? Why do people feel the need to wire uteruses for sound in an effort to teach fetuses, believing this will give them an advantage over the other babies from birth?

I know many parents and caregivers out there are actively avoiding all the shiny plastic, computer chip–embedded, trendy, hip-for-a-moment, overindulgent trappings that can accumulate when babies and toddlers enter their lives. I also know that many others only accumulate the stuff because they think it is necessary because everyone around them is doing it. I also know that babies have developed just fine for thousands of years without prenatal education systems and wireless color video monitoring systems mounted over their cribs.

Tasha and I had a lot of stuff we probably didn't need back in the early 1990s, when our two children were babies, but the more that we work with infants and toddlers, the more we realize we can do without. Babies and toddlers get lost (figuratively and literally) in environments with too much stuff. The child should always be the focus. Yet too often the focus turns to things. Quality infant and toddler care is not dependent on the quantity of baby stuff; it is dependent on the quality of relationships. To do right by our babies, we need to focus less on the amount of fancy stuff we accumulate and focus more on the actual child we have done all that shopping for. Cutting back on the stuff will reduce physical and mental clutter, save money, and provide more time to interact one-on-one with the actual child. We cannot let our attachment to things overshadow our attachment to people. Here are some questions to help you think about your stuff:

- How do the things I have purchased recently really improve my quality of life?

- What stuff could I get rid of to declutter my physical and mental space?

- What toys and equipment lead to conflict, chaos, and confrontations? Would life be better without those things?

- How much am I spending on stuff I really do not need? What would saving that money allow me to do?

Face-to-Face versus Face-to-Screen

> I'm lying on the floor with six-month-old Lilly. We are both on our
> sides, facing each other, gazes locked. We are face-to-face, and I
> see my reflection in the deep dark pools of her eyes as she clumsily
> attempts to mimic my facial expressions. She is skilled at sticking
> out her tongue when I do, but she is still mastering moves that are
> more complicated. As we continue with the face game, from above
> I slowly move my left hand into her line of sight. When she sees
> my wiggling fingers slowly moving toward her face, she twists for a
> better view and grins a wide toothless grin. Her arms reach for my
> hand, fingers pumping open and closed. A moment later, she grasps
> my index and pinky fingers and smiles at me with her eyes. I shake
> my hand, and her whole body gently rocks back and forth. Her
> entire face shines with delight. Our play shifts gently with our whim.
> The one constant is that our eyes are always on each other.

....

That is early learning at its simplest—two people connecting. Yet this
uncomplicated face-to-face contact gets replaced by face-to-screen contact more and more. The American Academy of Pediatrics felt so strongly
about the practice of putting babies in front of screens that in 1999 it
released a statement urging parents to avoid television and other electronic media for children under the age of two (American Academy of
Pediatrics 1999). We know that face-to-face time is better for babies than
face-to-screen time, but 25 percent of children under the age of two have
televisions in their bedrooms (Rideout, Vandewater, and Wartella 2003).
Lapware is a multimillion dollar industry.

The communication between a child and a screen is unidirectional;
the screen spits out images for the child to absorb. Face-to-face communication is multidirectional; the child and whomever she is interacting
with share information. This interpersonal exchange of information is
how humans are biologically predisposed to learn. The TV, computer, or
video game screens are unable to respond to the individual needs of a

given child, and children are not biologically disposed to interact effectively with screens.

Some people argue that computers and electronic media are a huge part of the modern world and that it is important for children to know how to interact with this technology. This may be true, but infancy and toddlerhood are not the right time. Most babies will one day need to know how to interact appropriately with automobiles, fire, water, and electricity, but we do not give them the car keys, light the car on fire, push them into a lake, and toss in a toaster to help prepare them for the future. Some babies are going to grow up and need to know how to operate chain saws and heavy equipment, but we do not give them access to these things in infancy. For their safety, we wait until they are developmentally ready to introduce these things. We need to do the same with computers and other media.

Choosing face-to-screen time for infants and toddlers builds habits that could last a lifetime. How bad is our addiction to screen time? More than once, I have seen children under the age of four climb inside a large cardboard box that could become a spaceship, car, submarine, doctor's office, or jungle hut with a smidgen of imagination only to see them pretend to watch TV, play video games, and pop in DVDs.

You have to choose what is right for you and the children you care for. Me, I'm going to go spend some face time with Lilly.

Here are some questions to help you refine your thinking about young children and screen time:

- How much time are you spending in front of screens, and how is it affecting your primary relationships?

- How would you invest your found time if you cut back on screen time?

- How do your real-life screen time habits gel with your beliefs about early learning, interpersonal relationships, and quality of life?

Living in the Moment versus Recording the Moment

Not only are our babies spending more of their early years in front of screens than any previous generation: they are also in front of the lens more than their parents or grandparents. Everything is chronicled with pictures and videos: pregnancy, birth, birthdays, trips to the park, trips to the zoo, first of this thing or that thing. Mundane or monumental, it is all archived somewhere. We seem to have a cultural need to document every-

thing. Our babies are also stuck in front of other cameras: video monitoring systems in homes and child care programs, nanny cams hidden in teddy bears, security cameras in stores, parks, and on city streets. Someone is always watching.

Some pictures here and some video there is not the problem. The problem arises when the need to capture events outshines the events; when the candles on the second birthday cake have to be blown out repeatedly to get the right shot; when parents only look at their children through a camera's viewfinder; when children feel like they are always on stage and have to shine; when life is put on hold until the batteries are changed; when a moment can't just be a moment but has to be a production. I've done photography for some of my books, and it is very difficult to get candid shots of children simply playing, because as soon as they see a camera, they stop being real and start posing. I remember a one-year-old who would drop everything and put on a phony smile every time she spied my camera.

Children need down time, and that is hard to find when you are always in front of a camera and expected to perform. We adults also need to realize that we are constantly missing chances to participate and interact with children when we seclude ourselves behind a camera. Our need to document life for later review steals opportunities to participate fully in life now. It is impossible to interact with a child in the present moment while simultaneously trying to capture the moment with a camera.

Here are some questions to ask yourself about how you choose to use cameras and video equipment:

- Are you balancing your time in the moment and behind the camera?

- Do you ever find yourself missing moments because you are busy trying to record them?

- Do you ever review or use your collection of photos and videos?

- Is being behind the lens easier than being in front of it or without it? Why?

Hope versus Fear

While the best interactions with infants and toddlers happen when the adult involved is relaxed, rested, focused, centered, in the moment, and free to fully be part of the exchange, our hectic and hurried lives often leave us more anxious than comfortably tuned in. We have plenty in our lives to be anxious and fearful about. We're bothered by what we can control and bothered by what we can't control. We worry about yesterday and we worry about tomorrow. We fret about choices made and fret about choices left unmade. We struggle with our personal ambitions and our lack of personal ambitions. We fear becoming our parents or we stress over not living up to the high standard our parents set. We also allow larger, darker anxiety and fear to seep into our relationships and interactions with infants and toddlers. We all carry our pasts with us. Sometimes those pasts are full of gloom we fear we will repeat or cannot completely overcome.

Any stress and anxiety we bring to our interactions with babies and toddlers reflect back on us. Children are biologically programmed for social interaction, and because of this, they mirror the emotions we bring to the interpersonal exchange. I know that when I let go of anxiety, I interact better with the children in my care. The exchange with Lilly I described a while back would not have worked if I had not been fully present with her, and I certainly would have responded differently to Hunter pooping on his hand had I not been relaxed and in the moment. It's a generalization, but relaxed adults raise relaxed children, and anxious adults raise anxious children.

The good news is that we can choose to deal more effectively with our own levels of stress and anxiety, hope and fear, so that they are not such a factor in our interactions with children. There are plenty of things in the adult world that scare me and cause me varying levels of fear and anxiety.

War, politicians, eroding freedoms, commercialism, money, groupthink, Space Invaders (the old Atari video game, not actual invaders from space), parenthood, marriage, and the future are just a few of the things that have caused me to stress out in the past twenty-five years. These things are way beyond the scope of understanding of the young children I work with, but any stress and anxiety relating to them that I carry into a caregiving situation will become obvious to even the youngest child. My daily routine involves yoga and meditation to help me let go of these fears and anxieties, to get my mind right, before I have contact with any children. I know parents who take the long way from work to their child care so they can decompress before seeing their children. Tasha likes to listen to music from the eighties while she works out to decompress and let go of the baggage she is carrying.

Healthy interactions with infants and toddlers must be built on a foundation of hope and joy; we should exude a positive and bright outlook as we introduce them to the world and its wonders. Our mind-set has a huge impact on our adult relationships, and its impact on our relationships with small children is even bigger. I am lucky enough to know many such caregivers who allow their hopeful attitudes to wash over the children in their care, shielding them from the often scary realities of the adult world. Children are drawn to these adults who shine with optimism and delight in life.

The sad reality is that the world is often a scary place, and fear just seems like common sense. It is only reasonable to be afraid when it appears the world around you is crumbling. All those things that cause anxiety and stress are realities of the adult world, and it is our job as professional role models to protect the children in our lives from those things as long as possible. The world is full of fear, but our job is to protect them from it. This means that we must learn to acknowledge our own fears and then let them go. Doing so is the only way we can truly engage infants and toddlers with a hopeful heart and joyful mind-set.

Dealing with your personal fears and anxieties in a healthy and consistent manner takes time and effort. The payoff, however, is worthwhile: you will feel more hopeful and more focused, you will experience more flow, and you will make better choices. Your interactions with children (and the rest of the world) will be more positive and fulfilling. Here are some common fears caregivers have and some tips for coping with them.

Fear of the future: There are valid reasons to fear the future, but instead of constantly focusing on those fears, consider changing your mind-set. When we expect bad, we will find it, but when we seek out good, that is what we will see in the world. Our default setting is to see the bad in the world, but with effort we can change our outlook.

Fear of messing up: This fear can be so powerful that it paralyzes some parents and caregivers, making it nearly impossible for them to move forward or make choices. If this is a fear you are facing, take a moment to think about why you are afraid to make mistakes. This fear may go way back to your own childhood. Knowing the origin will help you understand it and weaken its control over you. Realize that mistakes are part of everyone's life and that you will make your share. It's even okay to make and admit to mistakes in front of small children. Seeing that you are not perfect will actually be a relief and allow them to learn that mistakes are part of life, that it is normal to make them once in a while.

Fear of becoming/not becoming your parent(s): Many adults live in competition with their own parents. It is a fear that often exists below the surface. We either fear not living up to a high standard that a parent set or that we are destined to live down to the low standard with which we grew up. If this fear belongs to you, first take a deep breath and realize you are not your parent and there is no logical reason for this competition. Second, spend some time visualizing yourself letting go of this fear and doing your best in any given situation. You will make better choices as your own person if you allow this fear to fade away.

We'll end this section with some questions to help clarify your thinking about hopes and fears:

- What are you afraid of? (Take time to actually write a list. Physically holding this list in your hand will help you begin to deal with your fears.)

- What are you hopeful about? (Again, invest time in writing down your hopes.)

- Where do your biggest fears come from? (Do they have the same or similar sources?)

- What can you do today to live a more hopeful life?

Children's Needs versus Your Needs

Much of early care and education boils down to balancing the child's needs and your needs. If you focus too much on *either* the child's needs or your own needs, the relationship will flounder. It is all about finding balance.

Here are some examples:

- Infants develop just fine without ever being strapped into a swing or bouncy seat. In fact, not using this equipment might be in their best interest developmentally. Nevertheless, if the only way you can make time to clear your head every day is by placing the baby in a swing for a few minutes while you meditate or quietly drink a cup of tea, then use the swing. A bit of time in the swing won't damage the child, and your clearheadedness will make the rest of the day smoother.

- If everyone in your peer group uses disposable diapers, and your mother says disposable diapers are so much easier, and disposable diapers are less hassle, and you still want to use cloth diapers, use cloth diapers. You may have to deal with comments and looks from Mom and your friends, which might make you uncomfortable and self-conscious, but making the choice that is right for you in these situations is generally the right choice for your child too. If you feel one kind of diaper makes you a better parent, that choice is going to increase your confidence—and *that* will make you a better parent.

- You enjoy feeding your infant cereal and finger foods, but she is showing signs that she is eager to do it herself. She needs to develop her small-muscle skills, and you need to feel like you are taking care of all her needs. Start by following your infant's cues. Chances are you'll enjoy watching her feed herself, and she'll be happy to have you help after she has a turn feeding herself.

It is our responsibility to balance our relationships with children. We are the only ones capable of doing this. By default, the job falls on our shoulders.

Here are some questions to consider when questioning your balance one way or another:

- Am I investing time and energy in the things that really deserve my time and energy?
- What is my inner voice saying about the choices I have made recently?
- In this moment, am I at peace with the world or overwhelmed by the world?
- Am I physically relaxed, or do I feel tense and anxious?

If you find that you are losing or have lost your balance, the Taking Care of Yourself features in this book offer tools for finding it again. Taking time to use these tools will help center your mind and refine your focus, leading to better balance.

. . . .

TAKING CARE OF YOURSELF

Letting Go II

Here is a technique that will help identify the emotions and ideas you are hanging on to that might be influencing the quality of your choices and interactions with infants and toddlers. It will also help you start letting go of some of those things. Moreover, this technique is a great tool for keeping stress and anxiety from building. Use it periodically to clear your head of unnecessary, negative clutter. Read the following steps a few times and then try them out.

1. *Get comfortable.* Find a position that is relaxing and easy to be in. Sit, lie down, stand on your head—whatever works for you.

2. *Breathe naturally.* Simply let your breath come and go on its own. Don't try to control its rhythm or depth.

3. *Visualize.* Imagine all the things that you are holding on to—all your stress, anxieties, fears, frustrations, and all the rest—forming a ball that is floating in the middle of your chest.

4. *Acknowledge.* Name each bit of negativity as it becomes part of that ball. Take a moment to think about where it came from and why you are still carrying it around with you.

5. *Reach.* Look deep inside for hidden items to add to the ball. Sometimes they are crammed back in a dark corner of your mind. Sometimes you have to reach into your toes or fingertips to find them. Seek them out and add them to the ball.

6. *Feel.* Spend a few moments experiencing the feelings this imaginary ball contains. This can be tough because you have spent a lot of time pushing back these feelings.

7. *Let go.* Now, visualize that floating ball of negative energy evaporating into silky wisps of translucent steam that spirals out of your chest and into the atmosphere. Replace the weight of the ball with lightness and positive energy.

8. *Center.* Allow your mind to settle. Feel the lightness and positive energy permeate your body. Pay attention to your breath. When you are ready, return to your day.

Most of this chapter has looked at things like television, media, consumerism, fears, anxieties, societal pressure, and other big-picture issues that influence our one-on-one relationships with infants and toddlers. These macro topics can have a gigantic impact on the dynamics of adult-to-child interactions. All the choices we adults make outside our relationships with the children in our care manage to trickle into those relationships. We are often unaware that they are there, but their influence is felt when we try to tune in and lead the dance of early learning. If we carry too many big-picture pieces into caregiving, if we spend too little time thinking about big-picture issues and making mindful big-picture decisions, if we fail to acknowledge that there *is* a big picture, we inhibit the depth and quality of the relationships we form as well as the quality of the play, exploration, and discovery we are trying to foster.

After we deal with this big-picture stuff, we can focus on the small picture, the actual person-to-person relationship with a child. Effectively addressing the macro issues allows us to give our full attention to our moment-by-moment interactions. The small picture is the focus of the remainder of this book. The next chapter looks at creating emotional environments based on mindful and in-the-moment interactions with infants and toddlers.

≡☆

Chapter 3

Look Them in the Eye: Building Strong Emotional Environments

I can't dance. I'm an awkward bungler with two left feet made of lead. I can't salsa, disco, or polka. I can't samba, tap, or waltz. I can't line, slam, or square. I can't ballroom, river, or swing. I can't krump, belly, or modern. After years of bruised toes, my wife has banned me from attempting dance in public. My body and the music never sync. My feet fumble. I am rhythmically challenged, self-conscious, and clumsy. Light on my feet I am not.

Unless I am dancing with kids. They find my moves both entertaining and inventive. They see me as a free spirit moving to the sound of my own drum. They don't judge me when I attempt classic dance moves like Driving the Bus, Changing a Diaper, Pouring Milk, Fly Fishing, Haywire Robot, and my favorite, Eating Cereal While Standing Barefoot on Hot Concrete. Small children respect me as an artist.

I can't dance to music because I never had a reason to learn or a real interest. I have, however, spent the last two decades practicing the dance of child care. It holds my interest and fascinates me. The subtle flow of information between the dancers, the ability to predict based on prior knowledge and experience, the ebb and flow of emotions never fail to amaze me.

With a lot of practice, I have become respectable at the dance of child care. I can usually keep my mind in the room, read the signals I am receiving, and respond to them appropriately.

....

Two-year-old Annie flashes across the room, her eyes blazing and her brow furrowed. The light catches her gleaming white teeth as she nears her prey. She is a lioness. She is a wolf. No, she is a ravenous velociraptor ready to sink her teeth and claws into a cute little baby triceratops. In a stern voice reserved for such situations (a bit louder and deeper than usual), I say her name: "AAAAnnie!" She turns toward my voice, and our eyes connect. Instantly her forward motion stops, her brow relaxes, her claws retract, and those sharp teeth disappear into a closed mouth. She points to a toy the unaware baby triceratops is playing with and says something that sounds like "Mine." I hold out my arms, and she comes to me. "Mine," she says again. As she settles into my lap, I whisper gently in her ear that she put down the toy ten minutes ago. The baby is playing with it now. I suggest we find a different toy. She toddles to the bookshelf and returns with a dinosaur book that we read over and over.

....

Annie and I have been looking each other in the eye since she was a few months old. She came to us from a child care program with a caregiver who was unable or unwilling to perform the dance. Annie only spent a week or so in the program before her mother realized that her baby daughter was not getting what she needed. Because of our long history, Annie now knows that the tone of voice and look in my eye mean, "Stop, do not bite," just as well as I know her body language means, "You did me wrong, and now you will pay!" The emotional environment of our program makes it easier to prevent problems and move beyond challenging situations. Annie has become more than willing to trade the toy for some one-on-one story time.

When we adults move beyond the big-picture clutter and focus on small-picture relationship intricacies, the emotional environment works and play, exploration, and discovery flow. This chapter deals with the complex and intuitive dance between caregivers and babies, the intricate interplay of emotion, and the give-and-take of mental energy that is involved in creating strong emotional environments. The emotional environment supports infants and toddlers in developmentally appropriate play, exploration, and discovery. Early learning and the formation of strong attachments is not about all the big-picture things discussed in chapter 2. We adults need to make mindful choices about those things and then set them aside and focus on small-picture issues. We need to tune in to the little signals—often nearly imperceptible—that children send our way. We need to center on their needs in any given minute and not the needs of outside entities working to sway our thinking. We need to hold children in our arms, look them in the eye, and be completely present in the moment.

TAKING CARE OF YOURSELF

Finding Flow

The feeling of flow is also known as *optimal experience.* The term was coined by Mihaly Csíkszentmihályi, former head of the Department of Psychology at the University of Chicago, who has researched the experience of flow for years and written about it in *Flow* (1990), *Creativity* (1996), and *Finding Flow* (1997). In *Creativity,* Csíkszentmihályi defines flow as "an almost automatic, effortless, yet highly focused state of consciousness" (1996, 110). This is the state of mind in which we are best at doing the dance of child care, the state in which we are most able to move in step with a child. Csíkszentmihályi also identified nine characteristics of flow (1996, 111–13). Not all nine are needed to experience flow, but they are all commonly reported elements described by participants in his research.

There are clear goals every step of the way. Devoting time and energy to planning and goal setting helps chart a clear course of action and clears the mind of big-picture thinking.

There is immediate feedback to one's actions. When you are experiencing moments of flow, you are better able to tune in to the feedback received from children and better prepared to use that information in a thoughtful way.

There is a balance between challenges and skills. In a state of flow, you feel challenged, but you feel your skills are up to the task at hand. You are not overwhelmed or experiencing things you are not able to handle.

Action and awareness are merged. You are focused on what you are doing. Your mind is in the moment, not thinking about last night or tomorrow.

Distractions are excluded from consciousness. You are unaware of things that would normally distract you. You are aware only of what is important here and now.

There is no worry of failure. You are too involved in what you are doing to worry about failure. You know what needs doing and that your skills are most likely up to the task.

Self-consciousness disappears. In moments of flow, you are not concerned with what others say or think. You are so caught up in the moment that you forget to worry about the things that make you self-conscious at other times.

The sense of time becomes distorted. You forget about time when experiencing flow. Hours could pass in what seems like minutes, or a unique and special moment could seem as if it lasts a long time.

The activity becomes autotelic. *Autotelic* means that something is an end in itself. Most of life is exotelic because we do things to achieve some later goal or reward. Autotelic experiences are valuable in and of themselves.

In *Finding Flow* (1997), Csíkszentmihályi reports that most people experience moments of flow and that one in five Americans say it happens often, even multiple times a day.

Observe Basic Quality Standards

Strong emotional environments are constructed on a foundation of basic quality care. Much has been written about this topic, so we will only take a quick look at the most basic of the basics. For more information, check out *Prime Times* (Greenman, Stonehouse, and Schweikert 2008) and *The Creative Curriculum for Infants and Toddlers* (Dombro, Colker, and Dodge 1997).

Health and Safety

The physical environment should be clean and free of hazards. Infants and toddlers are curious creatures, and while they do not intentionally seek out ways to harm themselves, they are good at finding potential dangers. Physical environments should be examined for potential health and safety risks on a regular basis by an adult thinking like a curious toddler. Then changes should be made to abate those risks.

Group Size

It is probably no great surprise that resilient emotional environments form better in small groups than in large. We touched on this already, but I think it is important to repeat it: fewer children per caregiver makes the formation and maintenance of strong relationships easier. It's common sense: when adults are responsible for fewer children, they have less stress and are better able to dance the early care-and-learning cha-cha. Adult-to-child ratios for child care programs vary greatly across the country. Generally, one adult is allowed to care for up to four children under the age of two or up to six children ages two to three years old. Maximum group size is usually two caregivers in a room with eight to twelve children. Lower ratios are better.

Continuity of Care

Continuity and predictability in the day-to-day caregiving routine are important in building successful emotional environments. So is continuity in who is doing the caring. Imagine being six months old and unable to predict who will show up when you need your next diaper change or bottle. Having too many caregivers makes relaxing and feeling at ease

difficult for small children. It is best to limit the number of caregivers a child has during her first three years of life.

. . . .

TAKING CARE OF YOURSELF

Basic Meditation

Your mind-set has a huge impact on the emotional environment you create with children. The quality of your interactions and your decision making improve when your mind is clear and free of clutter. Meditation is a powerful tool for clearing and decluttering your mind. Some people shy away from the idea of meditation because they see it as a freaky, New Age, or countercultural activity, but the fact is that meditation has been part of human civilization for a long time. For thousands of years, people have used meditation to focus the mind, deepen understanding, and reduce stress. In fact, many of the world's religions had founding prophets who used meditation as a tool to find clarity. Mohammed, Buddha, Jesus, Abraham, and other prophets meditated. Some people believe that prayer is the way to talk to their god and that meditation is the way to listen for an answer.

While there are many advanced meditation techniques, you don't have to buy special robes, shave your head, move to Tibet, or learn to levitate a few feet off the floor. All you have to do is follow these basic steps:

1. *Be comfortable.* Most people are uncomfortable after a few minutes on a hard floor with their legs crossed and the backs of their wrists resting on their knees. Sit or lie in a position that works for your body. Don't force yourself into a position that causes you pain.

2. *Close your eyes or find a fixed place to rest your gaze.* If you are uncomfortable with your eyes closed, stare at a spot on the wall, a piece of lint on the floor, or your fingertips. The point is to cut out as much visual stimulation as possible.

3. *Breathe naturally.* Don't try to control your breath; let it happen. Be aware of how it feels as it enters and leaves your body.

4. *Allow your mind to still.* It probably won't want to be still. It is made to think, and it is used to being busy. If you try *not* to think, it will get even busier; you cannot force your mind to clear. What you can do is simply acknowledge the thoughts that pop into your mind as they appear, and then let them go. Imagine a stream flowing in front of your eyes, and imagine your thoughts flowing down that stream. When a new one appears, simply recognize it and then let it flow past. What we are seeking is the stillness between thoughts. Like developing any other new skill, finding this stillness takes practice.

5. *When you notice that your mind has wandered,* gently return to the image of the stream from the step above and begin naming and letting go of the thoughts that appear in your mind.

6. *When you are done,* take a few long and deep breaths and slowly open your eyes.

I have done this simple activity with thousands of child care providers and parents, and it is amazing to watch their body language as they are going through the process. In less than five minutes, their shoulders, foreheads, faces, jaws, and backs relax, their breathing slows and deepens, slight smiles appear on their faces, and the energy in the room mellows.

Finding five minutes a day to sit and practice these steps can do the same for you. It is a great way to take the edge off the stress that comes with life; it will allow you to better care for yourself and the young children in your life. It will build a more focused mind and improve the emotional environment you create for the children in your care.

The Sad Reality of Basic Care

Sadly, too many of our nation's children are not even getting the basics. I was reminded of this not too long ago. While taking a walk, I heard these words blasted at a two-year-old child: "Get back here! *Get back here!* Get back here *now,* you dumb little f_____!" The curly-headed blond child, clad only in a droopy diaper, was inspecting a grasshopper perched on a long blade of grass three feet away from the screaming woman. The child kept watching the bug, inching an extended index finger in its direction. The woman stomped her foot and yelled again. I flinched. The child didn't. The infuriated woman grabbed a limp arm and yanked the toddler up the stairs onto a porch cluttered with beer cans and trash bags. "Stay on the damn porch!" she yelled at the unfazed child before tossing me a "Mind your own business, a__hole!" I continued my walk.

This woman's horrible language and actions didn't faze me as much as the child's lack of response to it all. He was so used to this behavior that it failed to register. The woman's yelling, screaming, and stomping was so commonplace that it had become background noise to the child's attempts to know the world. Through it all, he kept watching the grasshopper.

I witness such poor adult behavior in airports, parking lots, stores, parks, and child care centers. People degrade, disrespect, and dehumanize small children anyplace and anytime for any reason. Take a moment and imagine being that curly-headed child in a sagging diaper, exposed to that kind of role model for your whole young life.

The word *nurture* comes from the same Latin origin as *nutrire,* which means to suckle or nourish. It means to rear, help bring up, foster, help grow, help develop, train, and educate. For our purposes, we will define *nurturing* as all the things we adults do to help prepare infants and toddlers to be residents of the world. This includes the physical environments we create, the words we choose, our tone of voice, the nutrition we provide, the example we set, the skills we teach, and so much more. It also includes *emotional* nourishment. To be nurtured is to be cuddled when you need cuddling; to be guided in the direction of your dreams; to be allowed to do it yourself when you are able; to be loved simply because you exist; to be pushed but not pushed too far or too fast; to be trusted as a competent human being; to be expected to live up to your abilities; to be helped to new heights when you are mostly ready; to be consoled when you fall short of a goal; to be encouraged to try again; to be helped along your own path; to be assisted in becoming fully you. Nurturing is something learned best through experience; if you received it, you will generally know how to give it. I saw no evidence that the child on my walk received much positive nurturing, and the sad reality is that the yelling woman probably didn't get much either.

· ·

TAKING CARE OF THE CHILDREN

Over the Dark Edge

The worst-case scenario for adults failing to care for themselves and make thoughtful choices is a trip over the dark edge. When stress and tension are allowed to build, when bad choices are made, when options seem limited, too many adults fall over that edge and do something harmful—or deadly.

My experience is that we adults don't talk about this topic much unless we are sharing our horror. We are more apt to chitchat about others who have fallen over this edge than we are to discuss our personal experiences in the vicinity of it. As parents and early childhood professionals, we are not comfortable sharing our experiences near the dark edge—at least not with anyone but our closest and most trusted peers. It's whispered about and gossiped about. We know it happens, we feel bad when it happens in our communities, and most of us also *know* it could never happen to us. Here are a few examples.

- It's a hot summer day and a harried mother forgets to drop her three-year-old son off at child care. The child dies as the heat builds inside the car.

- A young and inexperienced father left alone with his infant daughter can't get her to stop screaming. His frustration takes over, and he holds a pillow over her face to quiet her.

- A preschool teacher starts smoking marijuana on her lunch break a few times a week. She says it helps her relax and "takes the edge off."

- An overstressed and aggravated family child care provider snaps. She shakes a toddler until his little brain bounces back and forth in his skull.

- A center director has a few too many drinks before picking up a van full of children from school.

- A foster parent decides the best way to handle a troubled child is to lock that child in a large pet carrier so the child does not harm herself or the other children.

It is easy to dismiss the people who do these things as bad, evil people who intentionally set out to harm children, but that is probably far from the truth. The fact is that sometimes good, dedicated, loving, kind, gentle caregivers are driven over the edge, acting in ways that physically or emotionally harm children. Something may snap, and a child is harmed physically in an uncontrollable moment of tragedy. The frantic pace we maintain can overwhelm us and lead to bad decisions and potentially tragic mistakes. Other times the need to get away from stress leads people to activities that are meant to "take the edge off." Such escapes may work for a while, but over time, these activities can turn into addictions to drugs, gambling, or alcohol, which may put children at risk.

We do not talk about it, but I think most parents and caregivers have been to the dark edge at least once. I've been there.

- When I was a frazzled and stressed-out new daddy, I forgot my son in the car while I ran into a store. The fact that he was with me completely slipped my mind until I returned to the car. Luckily, it was a cool evening, and I was back in fewer than twenty minutes. Under different circumstances, the lapse could have been tragic.

- There were times when both my children were under five and their fussing drove me to the dark edge. I remember throwing a baby bottle out the window as we zipped down the interstate on a family trip. If I had had the kid in my hands, I don't know what would have happened. Luckily for everyone, their mother was available at these times to act as a release valve. I was able to mentally walk away from the situations and regain control. Not everyone has a release valve—or the presence of mind to know one is needed.

- In my twenty-plus years working with other people's children, troubled teenagers have threatened to shoot me in the back or smash my car windows, and crying infants have struck particularly annoying notes. These things, too, have made my skin crawl and brought me close to the dark edge.

This stuff is not easy for me to admit to the world, but if I can put my experiences out there, it might be easier for you to think about times you've approached your own dark edge and how you can keep from going over that edge in the future.

When you see the dark edge approaching, you do not need to make a 180-degree turn; you do not need to go from blowing fire and shooting lightning from your eyes to burping rainbows and dancing a happy jig. You just need to stop moving toward that edge. You need to slow down and turn enough so that you do not go over it. Here are some tips:

Walk away. Put some physical space between you and the child or situation that has brought you to your dark edge. Count to ten, take a few deep breaths, leave the room—do whatever you need to do to separate yourself from that edge. Also, make sure you make time in your life to recharge yourself—take a day off, invest some time in yourself, meet your own needs.

Have a support system. Have someone you can talk to openly about this topic. Someone you can call when you are having one of those days when you see your dark edge approaching. Have a release valve you can rely on in trying situations.

Know what brings you to the dark edge. Spend some time in your own head and know what brings you to *your* edge. Knowing what can drive you to the dark edge will help you avoid it.

Seek help. If you feel like you can't control yourself, know that it is okay to seek professional help in dealing with your situation. Admitting you need help shows strength, not weakness.

Be available. Support those near you who may be approaching their own dark edge.

The dark edge needs to be a topic that caregivers and parents talk about openly. Removing the taboo surrounding this topic will go a long way toward helping people recognize it exists and learning how to avoid going over it. We are not superhuman. We need to know ourselves, know what gets under our skin, and know that it is okay to ask for help when we need it.

. . . .
TAKING CARE OF YOURSELF

Setting Your Intentions

The first step toward accomplishing anything is having an intention. You don't get out of bed, buy milk, or have quality emotional relationships with the infants and toddlers in your life without first intending to do so. Every action starts out as a thought.

The problem is that life is so busy and you have so many outside entities trying to influence you that you often fail to put much thought into your intentions.

This leads to

- hasty choices that lead to swift actions so you can move quickly to the next thing.

- no time to think about long-term or big-picture issues, which means no clear intentions and no action.

Instead of making quick choices that don't give any real thought to day-to-day or big-picture issues, I suggest an alternative. Consider investing time regularly in setting your intentions for small and large concerns. This can be done with a variation on the meditation technique described earlier:

1. Get comfortable and rest your eyes.

2. Pay attention to your breath as it enters and exits your body.

3. Allow your mind to still.

4. After a few moments, begin visualizing some of the issues (large and small) that you have to deal with in your life. As you begin seeing these issues, take a moment to set intentions for handling them.

5. When you are done, take a few long and deep cleansing breaths, open your eyes slowly, and move on with your day.

What you are really doing is allowing yourself time to think, a luxury that most adults working with young children do not give themselves. This time for thinking permits you to be more intentional about your life, which leads to better choices, more thoughtful interactions with children, and a more thoughtful outlook on your world.

The Power of Nurturing

As caregivers and professional role models, we must see ourselves as nurturers. One of the most important things we can do is shower children with all the close physical contact they want. The cuddles and hugs and snuggles make them feel secure, safe, and loved. Those feelings are a good starting point for exploring the world. We must create emotional environments that promote learning and growth, environments that build on prior knowledge and biological realities. The rest of this chapter is devoted to the core components of a healthy emotional environment. If you observe the following principles, you will create emotional environments that work:

- Build attachments
- Understand temperaments
- Avoid overstimulation
- Make routines routine
- Do it again . . . and again
- Foster independence
- Let children lead
- Let them learn from their mistakes
- Tune in to tone
- Watch for clues and cues
- Acknowledge when the dance doesn't work

Build Attachments

We have established that young children need strong relationships with emotionally available adults in order to get the most benefit from play, exploration, and discovery-based learning opportunities. The conventional wisdom used to be that infants and toddlers only formed these emotional attachments to their mothers or a single, primary caregiver. We now understand that while the mother-child bond is usually primary, infants and toddlers can form strong attachments to multiple caregivers.

Forming such attachments takes time. I started chapters 1 and 2 with the births of my two children. While I felt connected to them from the moment of birth, forming attachments took time. We had to spend time together; we had to get to know one another. The formation of attachments takes time for new moms as well as new dads. There is a myth that mothers are magically attached to their infants from the moment of birth.

While biology generally helps make these attachments easily and quickly, it is a fallacy to believe they happen automatically. Healthy emotional environments don't just appear; they take time to develop and grow.

Attachments take time for nonparental caregivers too. Constructing a deep and meaningful emotional relationship with someone else's child is a huge investment of time and energy. Making good choices about big-picture issues and then setting them aside to focus on making yourself emotionally available, responding to clues and cues, looking children deep in the eyes and decoding what you see, understanding temperament, managing your tone, stimulating children without overstimulating them, and all the other things discussed so far in this book are colossal commitments. They are commitments that should not be entered into lightly. There are too many nonparental caregivers who do not take this job seriously enough. They do not understand the full impact of their influence and the importance of their job. They look at it as something to do until something better comes along. They look at it as babysitting. These individuals are cheating the children left in their care and diminishing a profession many of us take very seriously.

Investing yourself emotionally in other people's children is not only difficult—sometimes it is downright painful. I have had my heart broken a number of times. Children grow up, families move, parents' tragic lives and poor choices toss children about, abusers break bones and trust. When you share yourself emotionally with a child, you can end up sharing their hurts and sorrows. We once cared for a small child whose mother lived a life riddled with previous bad choices she was trying to outrun. We became the mother and child's only reliable support system, the only bridge not yet burned. We tolerated things from the mother for the sake of the child.

When the mother needed minor surgery, the only options for child care were us or a foster home. We agreed to do twenty-four-hour care for nearly a week. We took the child home when Mom was feeling better and received generous and heartfelt thanks.

We never saw or heard from them again.

These attachments carry very real emotional risks, but the rewards can be wonderful. Here's an example: two-year-old Annie's mom works in a National Association for the Education of Young Children (NAEYC)–accredited preschool program that does not operate in the summer, so after only five and a half weeks with us, Annie, her two older sisters, and Mommy spent a fun summer together. I anticipated Annie's return. We had developed a deep bond and were great dance partners. When I heard them coming up the front steps on the morning of her return, I positioned myself at the end of the entry, opposite the door.

Annie jumped from her mom's arms and rushed to me, her ponytail bobbing and bright white teeth exposed in an ear-to-ear grin. My heart leapt; she had missed me too. Her head nestled on my shoulder as we cuddled. Within minutes, she was off playing, returning to me for a hug from time to time. After twenty minutes, she shrugged her shoulders, turned up her palms, and asked, "Where's Mommy?" I told her Mommy was at work as she plopped down in my lap with a book. Someday Annie will outgrow our family child care program, heading off to school and her own life. We may stay in contact, but our later relationship will never have the depth it does now. She will leave a hole in my heart, but it will be worth it.

As a man, I have to tell you, it was hard for me to share this story. In fact, as a man it is challenging for me to work in the early childhood care and education profession. Out in the world, I get sideways looks from people when I tell them what I do for a living. Some think it is weird. Some assume I am a pervert or pedophile. Recently, I was talking on the phone to a woman looking for child care. She paused for a long time after I told her that my wife and I worked together. "You . . . you help feed them and change diapers and everything?" she asked. I replied that I did everything that needed doing and was fairly competent at it. She asked if I was ever alone with the kids. I explained that it happened frequently—sometimes Tasha needed to run errands or wanted to go home early. Then she called me a "sicko" and hung up.

I hear stories like this from other men in the profession. Some work in programs where they are hired for their gender and then not allowed to have any physical contact with the children. I've even met young fathers unsure about cuddling their own babies because they do not want to be accused of touching them inappropriately. Too many children in this country are growing up without positive male role models, and it is a shame that men willing to work as professional nurturers are seen as weirdos. If we want children to grow up and have healthy relationships, they need regular contact with caring, loving, nurturing role models of both genders.

Man or woman, it's hard to build these attachments, these bonds that will not last. Every time we enroll a new infant in our program, we say it will be the last. The emotional commitment is draining, and the investment of time and energy takes a lot out of us. Brenden was going to be our last baby. Then Lilly came along. Lilly was going to be the last one. Then Amy, Ty's mommy, happily announced she was pregnant, and we agreed to invest in one more new baby.

I received word from Amy that baby Emma would soon be making her appearance as I sat making notes for the conclusion of this chapter. Later in the day she arrived, weighing in at seven pounds and four ounces and measuring nineteen inches long. She has a full head of dark hair. Her aunt April assured me she was very cute, but I'll find out for myself very soon—we have to learn to dance together.

Understand Temperaments

Temperament is the unique traits that make up an individual's personality. My clearest understanding of it came during a weeklong WestED PITC (Program for Infant/Toddler Care) train-the-trainer session in Des Moines, Iowa, the second week of September 2001. On the tenth we

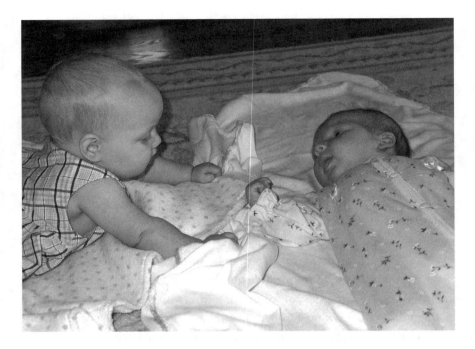

learned about the nine temperament traits and the three temperament types I describe below. On September 11, I started the morning watching the news, watching initial reports about a small plane hitting one of the World Trade Center twin towers, watching revised reports as new information reached newsrooms, watching the first tower fall. Later I watched my fellow attendees while we tried to continue the training, and then I watched other hotel guests in front of lobby televisions. Some cried; some didn't. Some huddled in small groups; some stood alone stoically. Some phoned home, some drank, some laughed nervously, some twisted napkins in nervous fingers, and some chewed the ends of pens. Some could not take their eyes off the TV screens; some could not bear to look at them. At least one longed to be home with his wife and two small children. You could taste and feel the stress in that hotel. Everyone felt it, and everyone reacted a bit differently, based on his or her personal temperament.

Understanding temperament makes the creation of healthy emotional environments easier because it allows you to tailor the environment to the needs of the individuals involved. Everyone falls somewhere on the continuum of each of the following nine temperament traits. Where we are located on each of the continuums determines which of the three temperament types we fit into. We'll look at them after reviewing the nine traits.

Activity level: Individual activity levels vary along a range from inactive to very active. Brenden, the four-wheel-drive child, is always in motion and ready for action, while other children I have cared for prefer stillness. Some babies wiggle and wriggle during feedings and diaper changes, while others are subdued during these activities. Some toddlers are doers and others are watchers.

Distractibility: Some people can focus on an activity while the walls shake and the roof falls in, and others are distracted by the sound of a butterfly's wings flapping a mile away. Distractibility refers to the effect outside stimuli have on an activity or behavior. The children you care for will fit on a continuum ranging from intensely focused to easily sidetracked.

Intensity: Infant or adult, some people experience their emotions more intensely than others. When they are happy, they are *very* happy, and when they are upset, they are *very* upset. On the other end of the spectrum, some people are much milder and more low-key in their responses to life.

Regularity: It seems odd, but you can set your watch by the regularity of some children's sleeping, eating, and pooping schedules. Others are habitually unpredictable and maintain no recognizable schedule or pattern whatsoever.

Sensory threshold: Sensory threshold relates to a person's sensitivity to physical stimuli. Reaction to textures, sounds, lighting, tastes, and other sensory experiences vary from person to person. Tags in clothing, fingernails on chalkboards, shredded wheat, bright light—things like these can cause strong reactions in highly sensitive people. Some of you probably cringed just reading the previous sentence.

Approach/withdrawal: Some people rush headfirst into new situations and interpersonal interactions, while others are more standoffish. Infants, toddlers, and their adult caregivers may be very willing to approach new people and situations quickly or may be reluctant and withdrawn, preferring to think and cautiously ease into anything new they encounter.

Adaptability: Some of us easily adapt to new situations, schedule changes, settings, routines, and people, while others abhor change. Transitions from one location to another or one caregiver to another can be difficult for some young children to handle. Others take to change like puppies to hot dogs.

Persistence: On one end of the spectrum are people who will start something and stick with it to the very end. On the other end of the spectrum are people who easily move on when they encounter an obstacle or gentle breeze. This means that some children will hate interruptions when they are engaged in a project, while others will move from project to project, leaving things incomplete.

Mood: This refers to an individual's tendency to react to the world in a primarily positive or negative manner. Some find it easier to be lighthearted, see the glass as half full, and be ever on the lookout for rainbows and cotton candy. Others are more serious, see the empty half of the glass, and suspect that a monster may be hiding behind the rainbows and cotton candy.

Before we move on, I must make it clear that the range of behavioral tendencies each of these nine traits cover is neither good nor bad—it simply is. It is okay to be shy and okay to be assertive. It is okay to be sensitive to scratchy fabric or loud noises, and it is okay to be oblivious to them. Recognizing where a particular individual falls in each of these nine ranges just makes it easier to understand and work with that person. Knowing that a child in your care is very active and needs ample opportunity to shake, rattle, and roll helps you create an emotional environment supportive of that child's needs. Not understanding this trait may leave that same child labeled as a "wild child" or "troublemaker."

It is also a good idea to identify yourself in each of these ranges and determine your own temperament type. Knowing these things about yourself makes it easier to interact with other people. For example, a parent who prefers order and a set schedule who has a child who is completely random in his eating and sleeping schedules will handle the situation better if she understands these traits. She will be better prepared to meet her own needs and the child's needs, and find balance in the relationship. In many ways Tasha and I are exact opposites, but because we understand these differences, we are able to live harmoniously.

Not understanding temperament traits can lead to confusion, blame, anger, and chaotic emotional environments. Expecting someone to behave counter to his or her innate traits is asking for trouble. Pushing an active child to sit still or a withdrawn child to quickly join a group is asking for trouble and creates an uncomfortable situation.

Take a look at the following temperament types, think about which one describes you, and decide where the children in your life fit. Knowing where you fit on each of the nine continuums I've described will help you figure out temperament types for yourself and others.

Easy or flexible: These individuals are generally calm, happy, and adaptable. They are not easily upset and have predictable eating and sleeping habits.

Difficult, active, or feisty: Individuals in this category find new people and situations scary, their eating and sleeping habits are irregular, and they are fussy and easily disturbed or agitated by noise and other sensory input. They are considered high-strung and intense in their reactions to the world.

Slow to warm or cautious: People of this temperament type tend to be less active. They withdraw and react negatively to new situations and stimuli. Given time and regular exposure, their reactions can become more positive. It takes time for members of this group to establish relationships.

Taking the time to understand temperament traits and types will serve you well in forming strong emotional environments. Knowing that the wild child who is always running around like the Tasmanian devil in a Bugs Bunny cartoon is not purposely trying to make you crazy and that the shy kid in the corner will join the group eventually if given the necessary support is helpful. Understanding and accepting your traits and the traits of others will make life easier for everyone. As Martha Stewart would say, "It's a good thing."

Avoid Overstimulation

Young children need stimulation, but too much of a good thing is a bad thing. They need chances to play, explore, and discover, but when their environments offer too many opportunities, children can shut down and stop participating. Infants will turn away and fall asleep if an environment offers too much stimulation. Another reason small groups are better than large groups is that they are less likely to be overstimulating.

Environments full of whizzing, dinging, donging, buzzing, blinking, shaking, rattling, rolling, whirring, whining, singing, talking, tinkling, zooming, glowing, flashing, clinking, and clanking toys, even if they claim to be educational toys, are not conducive to early care and learning. Blindingly bright, primary-colored walls covered in posters, pictures, alphabet letters, and cartoon characters are not appropriate for infants and toddlers. Shelves chock-full of too many choices make choosing difficult. Even the floors and ceilings in some early learning settings are covered with letters, numbers, geometric patterns, and too-bright colors. Poor babies, they have no place to rest their eyes. No calm. No serenity. No tranquility. In some settings, every item their busy eyes encounter has been turned into a misguided attempt to teach rather than an opportunity to learn.

I think even the *Sesame Street* people have gone too far. As if Tickle Me Elmo was not annoying enough, they went on to create the Elmo TMX! We needed another toy to overstimulate children and annoy adults? Shame on *Sesame Street* for selling out. Just because you can create and sell a loud, obnoxious, and overstimulating toy does not mean you should. *Sesame Street's* original focus on learning seems to have been lost to marketing, licensing, and just plain making money. Like many other once-trusted companies, I believe *Sesame Street* has sold its good name to the highest bidder.

Then again, most of us go overboard when it comes to creating environments for small children. The best thing we can do is back off and realize that when it comes to infants and toddlers, less really is more. They need environments that allow them to rest their eyes and their minds. They surely need stimulation, but we tend to offer them too much. Most care settings I have seen could back off on the amount of stuff, the brightness, and the whiz and whir by at least 50 percent. Early care and learning is not about flash and fluff, it is about focus; it is not about the quantity of stuff, but the quality of relationships.

Make Routines Routine

Building routines into your daily schedule creates a more comfortable emotional environment for young children. They enjoy the predictability and certainty of such a setting. You do not have to look far for routine either. In our community, emergency siren tests happen at noon on the first Monday of each month. Twelve times a year, the siren up the street bleats a test warning during lunch. The children cover their ears. Someone asks, "What's that?" Someone older explains that it is the first Monday of the month and the city is testing the emergency sirens. Then a discussion about what the siren is for, why it is so loud, and why it always happens during lunch takes place.

Another routine is garbage-truck-Monday. Every Monday morning between 8:30 and 9:30, the garbage truck makes its way through the neighborhood. The children love its loud engine, squeaky brakes, roaring hydraulic trash smasher, and the busy men toting the big green trash cans. If we are outside and the driver sees us, he blasts the air horn for our entertainment. Not tiny, wimpy, excuse-me toots, but big, obnoxious, get-out-of-my-way blasts that make little old ladies three blocks away spill their morning tea. The children wave and cheer. The smiling driver blasts the air horn again. On such days, that truck driver becomes a superhero to the kids in our care as he roars down the street in his powerful truck; he is Garbage Man.

If you're two years old, Monday at Jeff and Tasha's house is pretty darn exciting, but not all the routines we need to concern ourselves with are as loud and exciting as emergency sirens and garbage trucks. By their very nature, most routines are low-key and repetitive and lack excitement. That does not mean they are not important. In fact, routines are the bones of early care and learning environments. Routines provide the foundation for the day; they help events unfold in an orderly and predictable fashion. This is soothing to small children. It comforts them to know what to expect in different situations and to predict reliably what will happen next.

Here are some common daily routines:

• diapering

• feeding

• napping

- dressing

- story time

- outside time

- transition time

- cleanup time

- bath time

- bedtime

Other routines may take place less frequently:

- visits to friends or relatives

- religious services

- shopping

- neighborhood walks

- play with special materials like sand, water, or mud

Make these routines as predictable as possible. Doing so helps children know what to expect and helps them learn that the world is a predictable place. Making their days more predictable takes away stress and allows them to relax, making them more open to new experiences. A foundation of trusted routines sets the emotional groundwork for new learning.

Do It Again . . . and Again

Bendy brains need repetition. Repeated activities help to hardwire the connections between neurons that we discussed in chapter 1. Repetition is a building block of early learning. This is why children drop those darn plastic keys over and over for us to pick up. It is why they want to hear the same stories over and over. It is why they build, destroy, and rebuild the same block towers. It is why they examine toys, faces, and other objects again and again. They are building their brains.

I don't know what other authors do between writing paragraphs, but I like to play. In the little space between this paragraph and the last, I went and hung out with two-year-old Siddha. First, we played at sticking plastic faces and body parts on plastic potatoes. She worked hard at sticking the eyes, nose, ears, lips, hat, feet, and arms in the correct locations. Once a potato person was complete, she quickly pulled it apart and rebuilt. Repetition of this activity helps build her small-muscle skills, hones hand-eye coordination, and even solidifies her growing understanding of human anatomy. At just over the age of two, repeated contact with other people has taught her where eyes, noses, ears, and lips belong. I constructed a potato person with the arms in the ear holes, the ears in the arm holes, the lips and nose reversed, and one eye where the hat belongs, and Siddha chastised me with a "Nooooooo, Je" then took it apart and made corrections.

Our attention waned, and we moved to the kitchen to build with blocks. I watched as she repeatedly built towers of four blocks, one after another in a row. After completing five of these small towers, she took them apart block by block and rebuilt. Again, this repetition is helping develop her physical and mental skills.

We moved once more, this time to read books. I sat in our favorite reading spot, and she ran across the room to retrieve books. We went through six or seven picture books, each one twice. I would point at illustrated items and name them. She would repeat my words and point at the same item. We added oinks, meows, varooooms, and barks as needed and discussed items of interest in more detail. We always proceeded from left to right and from the top of a page to its bottom. We always made sure the illustrations were right side up. We always turned the pages with care. All this repetition added to her vocabulary, helped develop her ability to vocalize, ingrained reading skills and etiquette, improved her ability to visually discriminate between different items on the page, helped her small-muscle skills, and deepened our interpersonal connection.

Siddha also selected all the above activities and picked out all the books we read. Allowing her to have these kinds of opportunities to make choices repeatedly improves her self-image and helps her grow as a leader and decision maker. It gives her practice that will influence how she handles big-picture issues when she is an adult. She also picked up her toys and put away her books when done. Ingraining this type of repetitive behavior at an early age is a developmentally appropriate way to help her along the path to responsible behavior in adulthood.

The repetitiveness of our daily schedule also helps ground Siddha and the other children. When the days become predictable, transition times

are smoother and the children know what to expect. The emotional environment becomes comfortable and comforting when you know what is going to happen next, when the day unfolds in an unsurprising way. The schedule needn't be rigidly carved in stone, but major daily events should unfold in a knowable routine.

Repetition is indispensable in early learning, but it can really be a challenge for us adults. Finding flow amid all the repetition of our day can be difficult. Sometimes I feel as if my eyes will bleed if I have to read *Brown Bear, Brown Bear, What Do You See?* one more time. The repetitiveness of diaper changes, meals, nose wiping, transition times, and many other parts of a day with small children can wear on your nerves and leave you feeling more like you're stuck in the mud than flowing. Since we are the adults, we have to find ways to work through these moments of boredom and put our heads back into the dance.

Foster Independence

What nurturing does not mean is continuing to do things for children when they are developmentally ready and able to do things for themselves. While infants and toddlers are heavily dependent on adult caregivers to assure their health and safety as well as to nurture their social and cognitive development, they are also working from the very beginning to become independent entities. The whole purpose of the nurturing process is to help them develop into thinking, self-sufficient, capable, self-actualizing, joyful adults. Fostering independence at such a young age may seem counterintuitive to some people—they are just babies after all—but anyone who has spent much time with one- and two-year-olds knows they yearn for independence and desire opportunities to do things for themselves.

Fostering independence helps develop a supportive emotional environment because it helps you see the children as separate beings, view them as capable, and trust in their abilities. This does not mean toddlers should change their own diapers or be expected to cook their own meals. It does not mean expecting them to pay part of the utility bill and mow the lawn. It means taking little steps toward independence when they are ready for those steps. Here are some ways to help foster independence in infants and toddlers:

Help infants develop self-calming/self-regulating skills. When given a chance, most infants readily learn do things like calm themselves when upset, put themselves to sleep when tired, or turn away from the action when overstimulated.

Allow infants and toddlers to make simple choices. Let them choose which toy to play with or what activity to engage in. Older toddlers should be allowed to help pick out their own clothes. These choices should be simple. Holding two toys in front of an infant and letting her play with the one she reaches for is allowing her a choice. Giving a toddler a choice between three shirts allows him an easy choice, but sending him to pick one out of a drawer full of shirts may be overwhelming if he has not had practice. As infants and toddlers develop their choice-making skills, they can be allowed a wider range of choices.

Give toddlers responsibility. In our family child care program, once infants become strong walkers, they are expected to help pick up toys, carry their sippy cup to and from the kitchen at mealtime, and other simple tasks. Slightly older toddlers can help sweep, wipe tables, fold laundry, dress themselves, and do other household chores.

Provide toddlers with chances to manage their own time. Giving them freedom to spend time pursuing their own interests helps toddlers learn to manage that time wisely. It also helps them learn to entertain themselves. Too many children are caged in by rigid schedules that prevent them from gaining independence.

Simple activities like these build confidence and help develop life skills; they are a foundation for future independence. Sadly, too many young children do not receive such opportunities. I've met many four-year-olds unable to put on their own shoes or jackets and other older preschoolers incapable of simple self-care tasks. Opportunities to learn independence were stolen from these children in their earliest years, and it takes a lot of effort to make up for the loss. I have also seen independent and self-motivated children head off to school only to have that independence stripped by a school system that expects them to march though the school day in lockstep. Once-vibrant and self-motivated children return to us after a year of kindergarten unable to play on their own, expecting every moment of their day to be planned for them.

Fostering independence can be tough on caregivers for a number of reasons:

We like them to depend on us, need us, and look to us for support. Taking care of small children, doing for them, can be very enjoyable and provides a sense of purpose. It is often difficult to see them grow up. We want them to stay little and cute, and one way to do that is to keep them dependent.

Letting them do for themselves can be frustrating. They are inexperienced and lack skills, and that makes it hard for us to watch them fumble through tasks. Giving up or sharing control can also be very frustrating.

Fostering independence takes time. In our hurried worlds, it is often inconvenient to provide the time children need to do things for themselves. It is much easier to do it ourselves so we can move on to the next task on our long to-do list. For some people, letting children do things takes twice as long because not only does it take the child time to complete the task, but it takes the adult time to do it over "right" when the child is done.

Letting small children do things for themselves can also be messy. They spill milk, drop plates, unfold clothing, and make other messes in their efforts to do things on their own. Their limited abilities make it hard for them to perform up to our high standards.

We have to learn to deal with these problems and remember that our efforts to foster independence in infants and toddlers will have a lifelong influence on them and help them grow into adults who are not only independent but responsible, motivated, and capable.

Let Children Lead

From time to time, I still make the huge mistake of assuming that because I am older, more knowledgeable, and more experienced, I am supposed to be leading the dance. Doing so throws things out of whack. We adults need to remember that the child is leading the dance, and we are supposed to follow the child's signals. Here's an example of how I recently messed up.

Lilly, about four months old at the time, is lying on her back happily watching the world. She is perfectly content holding a wooden block and watching the older children play nearby. I should leave her alone; why mess with a happy baby? However, I have forgotten to bring my mind to work today and decide she needs some tummy time. I flip her over, tell her she needs time on her tummy, and arrange some toys in front of her. Lilly is not happy. Her upper lip quivers. Her eyes narrow to slits, and her forehead wrinkles. Then the crying starts . . . and continues . . . and keeps going. I can't console her. It takes a good fifteen minutes to help her return to her usual happy state.

In that moment with Lilly, I made a rookie mistake. I thought I was leading the dance. I thought I knew what she needed better than she did. The child's actual needs in any given moment are much more important than what we *assume* they need. If Lilly had been discontent on her back, watching the world, she would have made that fact known, just as she let me know I messed up with my ham-handed interruption. Looking back, I find it amusing that the reason for my misstep is that I was thinking more about writing this book than I was about my interaction with Lilly. I let the big-picture world leak into the small-picture moment I should have been experiencing with her. The child always leads the dance. Always. We adults will miss cues if our minds are not engaged, relaxed, fully in the room, and focused; quality care happens only when we are completely present.

Let Them Learn from Their Mistakes

Raise your hand if you have learned a valuable life lesson by first making a mistake.

Let me count.

Okay, that's everyone.

Experience is a great teacher, and sometimes the learning comes through a mistake. Sometimes we make the same error a few times before even realizing it is a mistake and that it is hiding something worth learning. Infants and toddlers are a lot like us. They also learn much about life from trying things, blundering, and then changing tactics in an effort to achieve a desired outcome. I have seen many toddlers between the ages of one and a half and two learn that tossing a tantrum is a great way to achieve a desired outcome with some adult caregivers. Their misstep is putting their whole body into the tantrum. They tighten their fists, cry, fall to their well-padded bottoms, and throw themselves backward onto the floor, hitting the backs of their heads. With time, each of these children learns that angrily falling backward and hitting their head hurts. Soon after this realization, they revise the process. They learn that plopping to their bottoms and gently lowering themselves onto their backs to continue their fit in full force avoids the bumped head. They also quickly learn that the whole give-me-what-I-want-or-I-will-throw-a-tantrum tactic does not work with some adults, and they revise their approach.

Our job as caregivers creating strong emotional environments is to allow them to make developmentally appropriate errors safely. We can't let them learn about fire, vicious dogs, and electricity through mistakes, but we can allow them to make innocuous mistakes that promote social and cognitive development. Learning to sit in a chair may require falling out of the chair a few times. Learning to drink from a cup may mean spilling some milk. Learning to put on their own shoes may mean getting them on the wrong feet the first fifty or a hundred tries. Learning to use the toilet may come with some bad aim and a few misfires. Adults who free children to make mistakes and realize that mistakes are a part of normal development create a more relaxed and comfortable emotional environment. Such environments are less stressful for small children and make it easier for them to build on their prior knowledge and experience. These mistakes are not really mistakes at all. They are part of the natural trial and error of early learning. They are strategic attempts to understand how to live in the world. They are part of the learning process and should be looked upon as opportunities for growth.

Unfortunately, when most of us adults think *mistake,* we also automatically think about all the negative baggage the word carries. We think things like *wrong, sub par, falling short of the mark, deficient, lacking,* and *poor.* We flash back to elementary school papers corrected in red pencil. We replay the uncomfortable feelings associated with our own errors in judgment. We stir up all the muck and gunk connected to society's antimistake mind-set. From there, it is only a skip and a jump to doing everything for young children in an attempt to keep them from making any mistakes, pressuring them to avoid mistakes, or blowing up at their errors. All this to avoid the emotional muck and uneasiness associated with making mistakes.

I've seen too much adult crying over spilled milk, scolding about right shoes on left feet, eye-rolling over upside-down books, and yelling about minor missteps. These actions send negative ripples through the emotional environment we are supposed to be creating for young children. The best thing we adults can do is take a breath, leave the emotional baggage associated with mistakes at the door, and remember that errors are a healthy and appropriate part of the early learning process. We make a big mistake if we take their little mistakes too seriously.

Tune in to Tone

The tone of voice we use with infants and toddlers is as important as what we say and do. The harshness of the woman cursing at the inquisitive toddler I described earlier in this chapter has no place in a healthy emotional environment. Her public display was an extreme, but it is easy to let the stress, tension, and frustrations from our big-picture adult world seep into our interactions with children. Your voice is a powerful early care and learning tool; use it to create the appropriate feel in your care setting. Relaxed, calm, low voices are much more effective than their harsh, shrill, piercing counterparts.

Babies and toddlers like soft, comfortable, singsongy tones. Many men accidentally upset children of this age with their naturally deeper voices. I have to purposely adjust my voice when talking to small children to make it more pleasing to their sensitive little ears.

Louder, deeper, sterner tones do have their place and can be quite useful when used appropriately and sparingly. They come in handy while claiming the full attention of toddlers approaching danger. A well-spoken "No" or "Stop" can freeze children in their tracks if they wander too close to a stove, street, or vengeful character wielding a laser sword.

Reserve this voice for when it's really needed. Too many curious toddlers out happily exploring the world do so under a constant barrage of shouted warnings, orders, and threats. The overuse of this tool turns it into background noise and diminishes its impact. The berated child watching the grasshopper was wholly desensitized to the harsh tone of his adult caregiver. On the other hand, the hair stands up on the neck of one of our child care moms when she thinks about her father's Daddy Voice because he used that voice so judiciously when she was young.

Know the power of your own voice and use it wisely. It is a valuable tool.

Watch for Clues and Cues

Earlier in this chapter, I shared how I messed up the early childhood dance with Lilly by flipping her onto her tummy when she was contentedly lying on her back, playing, exploring, and discovering. I not only missed her clues and cues, I completely ignored them, because in that moment I mistakenly believed I knew what she needed better than she did. I thought my experience was more important than her signals. After all, I have worked with hundreds and hundreds of children over the years. I have read many books and written a few. I have taken classes, attended conferences, talked with experts, perused pamphlets, studied articles, and sought out other information on child development. All my knowledge and experience indicated it would be good for lovely little Lilly to spend some playtime on her tummy. I was right too: tummy time is important for infants.

Except, that in that particular moment, I was wrong. All her signals said, "Please leave me alone. I am content." All of my experience, all the information from the experts, and every bit of research on child development were useless in that moment because I failed to read the clues and cues she was sending my way. Individual children know their specific needs and relay them to us through body language and verbalization. They are constantly communicating their likes, dislikes, wants, and needs through subtle and not so subtle expressions, movements, and vocalizations. Our job is to decode the messages they are sharing.

This is not an easy task. We need to focus on the dance in order to receive and respond to the clues and cues children send and to decode them based on the context and subtext of the exchange. This requires more than a basic working knowledge of child development. It requires that we know the child as an individual; that we understand her temperament; that we tune in to her moods and the moods of her other adult caregivers; that we know when she last ate, slept, and pooped; that we have a general idea of when she will need to eat, sleep, and poop again—that we are in the moment.

It would be so much simpler if children were born able to talk and verbally name what they needed in any given moment. Instead, we are stuck with deciphering their clues and cues. If Lilly scrunches her face and makes a particular whiny, grunting sound ten to twenty minutes after she arrives at our house in the morning, it means she wants a bottle. If she makes the same face and sound an hour or two later, it means she is ready for a nap. A very similar face and vocalization mean she wants a different toy or a change of scenery. Her eyes glaze when she is tired. Legs wildly kicking up and down like a frog mean she is very happy to see someone or something. She sucks her bottom lip to soothe herself. If she sees me and wants to play, she makes the cute little squeak followed by the frog leg thing.

I can read her clues and cues pretty well right now, and as she grows, they will change. This means I am constantly evaluating my understanding of her messages and updating my responses to her cues. Most children start talking sometime around the age of two, but they are communicating with us from the very beginning through other signals they send. To do the dance well, to create strong emotional environments, we need to know how to read and understand those signals.

Acknowledge When the Dance Doesn't Work

Try as we might, sometimes the early care and learning dance isn't so graceful. Sometimes strong emotional environments are too hard to create or sustain between a particular adult and a particular child. As the adult, if I am unable to tune in to a child and provide him the emotional support needed for play, exploration, and discovery-based learning, I need to make changes. Sometimes certain children and adults just do not fit together. Their temperaments may be too different (or too similar), their personalities may clash, or there may be an unnamable something that just keeps the relationship from working. This is okay; sometimes it happens. Not every adult caregiver is able to meet the needs of every infant and toddler.

When it does happen, we cannot ignore it. A parent unable to dance with her own child needs to seek outside resources and support. Asking for help when you need help is a sign of strength, and it helps your child learn that she, too, can ask for help. Other caregivers who find themselves struggling or are unable to give a child needed support should take steps to seek assistance or make it known that they can no longer provide care for that child.

It is also important that we look for other alternatives when the relationship between a parent and outside caregiver do not work. Strained parent-caregiver relationships have a direct impact on the interactions both those adults have with the child/children involved. If the adult's relationship cannot be made to function, the caregiving relationship should end.

. . . .

TAKING CARE OF THE CHILDREN

...And Then There Was Anthony

This story was written by Renae Boehmer. Renae is a former family child care provider who will eternally recall those thirteen years as her favorite time in the workforce, and the most meaningful. In addition to creating hundreds of baking soda and vinegar volcanoes and making up more silly songs than anyone has a right to, she has had time to care for three children of her own (currently fourteen, twelve, and eight years old), coordinate the nursery at her church, volunteer extensively in her community, and scrapbook a lifetime of memories. Renae received her degree in psychology from Augustana College in Sioux Falls, South Dakota, and currently works as a family life educator at Sanford Health.

New babies are a blast, aren't they? They stay where you set them down, they smile at just a few words of chatter as you walk by, and they love watching the big kids play. You can almost see the little wheels turning in their heads: "Soon I'll be able to run around like that—then I'm going to get those blocks and chew them all up!" They go from lying in the bouncy seat to sitting in the high chair to creeping along the floor, eyeing the toys that the older kids have out. Oh, to be so content.

But of course there are a few exceptions. I'll share one of mine with you. In my thirteen years as a family child care provider, I had only a few infants who really challenged my abilities and my patience. And then there was Anthony. He challenged my strength to go on. He challenged my super-patience. He challenged my eardrums. He challenged my knowledge of child development. I was a weary person at the end of many days with Anthony. I get tired even thinking about him now.

Anthony was what many child development specialists would refer to as "intense." He had "a lot of energy in his emotions." He was also persistent and active and sensitive. He liked to be held. No, he demanded to be held. He couldn't go to sleep unless you were holding him—and it was quiet in the room (something that didn't happen with enough regularity at my home to keep him well rested). He couldn't stay asleep unless his blanket was on his cheek and he was swaddled and the room was the right temperature (and I think there may have been some requirement about the planets aligning that he couldn't fully explain to me yet). He also had trouble coping with life if he was tired, meaning that he didn't eat much or enjoy having other children near him during those times, which turned out to be *most* of the time.

Yup, the blood pressure got high sometimes in those days. But I look at not-so-little Anthony now and I laugh at how much power such a little baby had on a full-grown, fully registered and certified child care professional. This child now has a wonderful vocabulary to express his feelings and adults who listen to him and are helping him control his intensity instead of letting his intensity control him. This child now goes to bed with a simple "G'night, Mama!" each evening without a care in the world.

So, how did we get from there to here? It took:

Patience. I knew *every* time Anthony cried that it wasn't about me. It wasn't a complaint or naughtiness that was causing it. He was an infant with a need, and it was my job to help figure it out and meet the need when I could. When that wasn't possible, I could be the calm force he needed in order to be able to fall asleep exhausted after crying.

Communication. Because of his sensitivity, he required consistency between home and child care. Constant communication with his parents helped us both meet his needs more consistently and help him learn that he could trust both of us.

Ear plugs. As someone sensitive to noise, I am aware that incessant crying is one of my triggers. Whether it was temporarily putting in some ear plugs or putting Anthony in another room to get a break, I knew I had to take care of myself first in order to have something left to give to him.

A Parental pact. I had an agreement with Anthony's mom (who struggled in the same ways I did) that I could call her at *any* time during the day to come and get him if I felt I was getting too close to the edge of my sanity. I never had to actually do it, but it felt good to know that I had an out if I felt like he was pushing me too far. But it was a two-way pact. She also had the right to call me any evening or weekend if he was pushing her too far. What more support could you want than that?

Prayer. Sometimes it's very freeing to realize that you aren't in control of every situation—and that you can ask for help when you need it. Giving up your feelings of inadequacy to God means that you are given a gift of God's power to help you find the answers you need.

Support. If I hadn't had a friend to call in the middle of the crying fits or when it was the third napless day in a row, I'm not sure I would have made it. I needed someone who understood my situation without judging my feelings.

As I said, Anthony is a big boy now with a bright future. He taught me a lot. He changed who I am. Every time I think of him, I remember the challenges, and I thank God for working through Anthony to make me a better child care provider and human being.

It's tough walking away from relationships that do not work. I have had to do it in the past, and I felt like a big stinking failure each time. I got over it with time every time because I knew it was the right choice—a hard choice, but the right choice. Making the hard choices, looking infants and toddlers in the eye, developing strong emotional environments, and the other topics covered in this chapter are all important building blocks in a solid early learning foundation. Learning happens easily when young children receive nurturing, respect, and love. These things empower them to know the world through play, exploration, and discovery. Investing time in building healthy relationships early on is not just the right thing to do for a child's emotional well-being; it is also an investment in future learning.

The next chapter builds on this foundation of respect and strong relationships and looks at how you can promote early learning with the infants and toddlers in your life.

Chapter 4

Learning through Play, Exploration, and Discovery

The easily observable fact is that children are passionately eager to make as much sense as they can of the world around them, are extremely good at it, and do it as scientists do, by creating knowledge out of experience. Children observe, wonder, find, or make and then test the answers to the questions they ask themselves. When they are not actually prevented from doing these things, they continue to do them and to get better and better at it.

—John Holt, *Learning All The Time* (1989, 152)

....

Play is not a luxury but rather a crucial dynamic of healthy physical, intellectual, and social-emotional development at all age levels.

—David Elkind, *The Power of Play* (2007, 4)

When you are dead, you have to stay dead. That's the way my cat did it.

—Phoebe, almost three, explaining how to
play dead to a friend during dramatic play

....

Making good choices concerning children in the big wide world and setting the stage with strong emotional environments in our smaller caregiving settings leads naturally to learning through play, exploration, and discovery. Young learners are scientists, explorers, inventors, thinkers, philosophers, engineers, theorists, linguists, seekers, mathematicians, artists, logicians, truth seekers, dreamers, discoverers, visionaries, and futurists. A biological drive pushes them to know the world, to define it for themselves, and to define their place in it. They will make this quest for knowledge to the best of their abilities in the worst of environments, shunning thunderous screams from inept caregivers in order to understand grasshoppers a bit better, or learning to roll, sit, walk, and talk in settings that offer little stimulation. Children's biological drive to learn is so strong, so adaptable, and so resilient that most infants and toddlers are able to overcome roadblocks, hiccups, detours, and diversions in their physical and emotional environments. The drive to learn is so strong that they do it in spite of their environments when they have to.

In the quality caregiving settings we create, it can be magical when we adults leave our baggage at the door and truly tune in to participating in the dance a child is leading. Early in chapter 3, I described dancing with Siddha as we moved from activity to activity. Caught up in a current of learning, we relaxed and allowed it to carry us from one learning opportunity to the next. We were in a state of flow: feeling capable of meeting the challenges of the task at hand, focused on what we were doing, tuned in to the moment, performing at the peak of our abilities, and deeply absorbed in what we were doing. All our work at making good choices and creating healthy emotional environments pays off in the flow moments of play, exploration, and discovery. Our job is creating opportunities for young children to have optimal experiences. If we have done the groundwork correctly, early learning is simple: support the child as he or she interacts with the world through play, exploration, and discovery.

I saw a great example of this one evening in a family-owned Korean restaurant in Minneapolis. It was near closing on a Friday evening. In a back corner booth, three teenage boys sat playing cards as a pair of young children bobbed and weaved their way over, under, and around the table. It was soon apparent that these kids were the children of the restaurant's owner and staff. Every now and then, the teenagers let the toddlers play a few cards. The energetic youngsters were constantly chattering and singing to the older boys. If the tots became too loud or wild, a glance from one of the boys was all it took to bring order. After a while, the card game ended, but the play continued. The teens began tossing cards to the toddlers, who tried to catch them in an outstretched cloth napkin. Then the tallest of the teens started lifting the toddlers up so they could touch the ceiling, gingerly pushing at the drop ceiling tiles.

Soon after, the teenagers left and the toddlers settled down in the corner booth again to play cards on their own. They were joined minutes later by a server with a basket of napkins. One toddler abandoned the cards and began dutifully assisting with napkin folding. Napkins were carefully folded and handed to the server. She smiled, thanked the child, and covertly refolded them. When they were all folded, the server kissed the child on the head and lavished him with more thanks while he returned to the cards and his companion.

There was a lot of learning going on in this play: language, hand-eye coordination, number recognition, social development, large- and small-muscle development, cause-and-effect thinking, problem solving, and much more. All of those things happened so easily because the environment was right. The children and adults were comfortable and tuned in to each other. It looked like kids goofing around in a restaurant—and it was—but it was also play-based learning at its best. The teenagers responded to the toddlers in a more fluid and thoughtful manner than some professional caregivers I have observed. They were not out to make the little ones learn anything; they just responded thoughtfully to the clues and cues they received. They were teaching and did not even know it.

Play, exploration, and discovery-based learning falter when the focus is misplaced. The focus should always be on the processes of play, exploration, and discovery. When we shift the focus away from these things, we get off track. Focusing on learning—the product of play, exploration, and discovery—is misguided and pulls our minds away from the all-important process of play. We also should not get too wrapped up in our role. I've met too many caregivers who feel that they are the center of a child's learning universe because they are a teacher. The focus revolves around what they are doing to make learning happen. The best teachers set the stage and then fade into the background, making themselves available when needed. We have to remember that we are not leading the dance.

. . . .

TAKING CARE OF THE CHILDREN

Dangerous Play

Health and safety always come first in infant and toddler care. We have to create and maintain physical environments, policies, and procedures to assure these things. Small children's unwavering drive to explore the world can quickly put them in dangerous situations. They act like superheroes, but they are fragile, inexperienced, and thoughtless. As their adult protectors, we must always be on the lookout for immediate and potential danger.

That said, sometimes we take safety too far. Some environments are too safe. Sometimes small children need to interact with materials that are potentially dangerous. They need to handle little bits and pieces that they can put in their mouths and they need to climb on things from which they can fall. Exposure to these potential dangers is important for the development of small- and large-muscle skills. Children who do not have opportunities to handle small objects and climb have a hard time developing the skills needed to

- write with a crayon, marker, or pencil
- snap, button, and zip clothing
- tie, buckle, or fasten shoes

• climb up stairs, into bed, or down from a chair.

I have met kindergartners who were kept overly safe as toddlers and ended up struggling in school because they did not have the small-muscle skills to hold a pencil properly, snap their pants after using the bathroom, or zip their own jacket. Their environments were kept so safe that they did not have opportunities to hone skills needed for school.

We need to seek balance. We need to find safe ways to let young children play with small bits and pieces and climb like little goats. This is not that difficult when we are tuned in and doing the early-care-and-learning dance to the best of our ability. When we are fully engaged and in the moment—not busy thinking about yesterday or tomorrow—it is easy to make sure this kind of play happens safely. We just need to be alert and focused on what's happening.

If you're looking for ideas for this type of play, check out my books *Everyday Early Learning* (2008) and *Do-It-Yourself Early Learning* (2006) or visit Lisa Murphy's Web site, Ooey Gooey, at www.ooeygooey.com.

Respect as the Basis for Learning

Emmi Pikler and her student Magda Gerber are the mothers of respectful caregiving. Their work focused on valuing infants and toddlers as thinking and capable individuals. Their observations and insights into caring for babies can be crystallized into six key principles:

• Observe more.

• Do less.

• Buy less.

• Support free exploration.

• Allow children to have control.

• Focus on self-dependent development.

(Gerber 1997)

Let's take a look at each of the principles and the ways they support early learning.

Observe More

Respectful care revolves around careful observation of the child as an individual. Spending more time observing will lead to more meaningful interactions and more thoughtful care. Take the time to know how small children act and react as distinct and separate individuals. Time spent observing furthers our understanding of temperament, developmental windows, emotional needs, and other traits that make following their lead in the dance of early care and learning easier. As observers, we also need to be on constant lookout for health and safety issues and developmental delays so that we can act quickly when needed.

Do Less

Our tendency as adults is to rush in and do things. We feel useful and important when we are busy fussing with this and fixing that. Pikler and Gerber recommend that we fight this urge (Gerber 1997). Our busyness takes the focus from the child and steals learning opportunities. Stepping back and doing less allows small children to build confidence and competence. It also allows us more time for observation.

Buy Less

As I described in chapter 2, infants and toddlers do not need all the toys, gizmos, and gadgets with which we surround them. Too much stuff hinders natural development, takes the focus off of the child, and clutters the environment. When it comes to baby toys, devices, and doodads, less really is more.

Support Free Exploration

Allowing small children uninterrupted opportunities for free exploration of their environments is developmentally appropriate. This time and freedom allows them to create their own learning curriculum. It also gives them control and power. Too often, we force our interests and inclinations on children and do not trust the children to be competent decision makers.

Allow Children to Have Control

Infants and toddlers should be given as much control and autonomy over their interpersonal interactions as possible. Too often, adults force their attention on children, showering them with silly faces, odd noises, and jarring jiggles to the point of overstimulation. We turn into entertainers putting on a show. The problem is that they are captive audiences who may prefer quiet time to a three-ring circus. Allow all children to determine when interactions start and end as well as the content of those interactions. Do this by tuning in to their clues and cues and really pay attention to what they are telling you.

Focus on Self-Dependent Development

Adults, particularly American adults, have a tendency to push and prod even the youngest children to develop. Instead of trusting babies to develop the skills needed for walking, we use molded seats and baby gyms and place them in sitting and standing positions in an effort to help them learn what millions of babies have learned naturally, at their own pace, and without the gizmos. Respect children enough to trust their abilities and let them drive their own development. Getting out of the way and letting them do their thing is one of the best things we can do to support early learning.

It takes time and energy to give infants and toddlers the respect they deserve. They are human beings—not possessions, toys, or objects. If we want them to grow up and act respectfully, we have to ensure that they know what respect looks like from their earliest days. Magda Gerber began working with Emmi Pikler because Dr. Pikler was kind and respectful to Gerber's daughter when they visited her office. All children deserve that kind of respect from adults.

· ·

TAKING CARE OF THE CHILDREN

Quality Children's Books

All children's books are not created equal. Too many of the books on the market for young children are written and published as part of the marketing and branding strategy for licensed characters or products. The idea is that children will see images of these characters or products in their books, on their clothing, on their diapers, on their birthday cakes, on their wallpaper, and on their sippy cups and become loyal to the brand for life. Many of these characters and products have been around for a long time; the marketers hope parents will buy them because of their own fond youthful memories. These books are created with strict oversight from the owners of the characters or products to assure that branding is maintained. The actual quality of the story and illustrations is not given as much thought as product placement. They are often written on commission by authors who receive no royalties or copyright for their work or by editors in the publisher's office to keep costs down. These books sell well, but their value as learning tools, let alone quality children's literature, is at best suspect.

When purchasing books, be wary of titles that promote popular cartoon characters, candy that will not melt in your mouth, or ties to movies or DVDs.

If you want quality children's books, look for books that have the following attributes.

Rich, inviting, and detailed illustrations. The pictures are as important as the words in a book for small children. Some wonderful books don't have any words at all. They simply rely on beautifully detailed and intriguing pictures to tell their story.

Text that you will enjoy reading over and over again. Quality books will use language in vivid and fun ways. Creating this kind of text takes time and effort. This is a luxury authors of low-quality books seldom have.

The name of the author and illustrator on the book cover or copyright page. The authors of low-quality books generally do not want or have the opportunity to be associated with their work.

Award winners. Type the search phrase "Caldecott Medal Winners" into your favorite search engine, and you will find a list of award-winning, quality children's books.

Quality books cost more, and you probably won't find them in the checkout line of your favorite big box store, but they are worth the investment. You will also find a wonderful selection of quality children's books at most libraries. Informal book exchanges with other parents or child care programs is another way to save money and expose the future reader in your life to a wider selection of books. Wherever you find quality children's books, know that their well-crafted stories, unfolding through rich illustrations and vivid words, will draw in listeners. Children will enjoy them more than the licensed character-driven books that dominate the market. Better yet, you will enjoy reading them more, and if you are going to read something thirty times in a row, it had better be enjoyable.

Integrated Learning

Infants and toddlers are always trying to wrap their bendy brains around new information. However, they do not have the capacity to classify their learning, discoveries, and new understandings as efficiently as we adults do, nor do they have the capacity to focus their learning very sharply yet. They seem to learn everything all at once as they play, explore, and discover.

Siddha is wearing a small ring of plastic pop beads around one ankle, enjoying the clunking and clanking as she walks back and forth across the room. "Siddha, try both feet," I suggest. She flashes a lightbulb-over-the-head look and proceeds to place both feet into the ring. All ten of her two-year-old toddler toes slide into the ring; it hangs loose on her ankles.

"Can you walk?" I ask. Her eyes flash again. She works her way to her feet, tries to take a normal step, and falls to her well-padded bottom. Determined, she carefully stands again. This time she changes tactics, choosing foot shuffling over normal steps. Her blue eyes dance as she slowly makes her way across the room, turns, and starts back to me. She tries to go faster and falls again. This time she gets up more quickly and decides to walk the rest of the way to my lap backward. Her head and upper body twist to the side as she charts her course. She plops into my lap, removes the bead ring from her ankles, smiles, and says, "Did it!"

....

This little scene played out in fewer than five minutes. Siddha was playing, exploring, and discovering, but she was also honing her language skills, practicing her logical thinking and problem solving, thinking creatively, building social skills, and improving her physical skills. Her curiosity drove her to try what I suggested. Her trust in me boosted her confidence; she knew I would not ask her to attempt something beyond her abilities. Her brushes with gravity pushed her to refine her movements and made walking work with the ring around her ankles. Walking backward was a creative flourish tossed in at the end to push her skills and impress us both. She paused in my lap for a few minutes to celebrate her accomplishment. Then she went off to acquire more knowledge about how the world works, knowing I was there to support her and prod her along when needed.

Infants and toddlers learn a lot of stuff all at once when they interact with adults, and they learn bunches from their interactions with older children too. For example, Noah, almost four, was playing house with Marygrace, almost two, at our house one day. He had mastered this kind of play, and she was a novice. During their play, he gave her some of his rich vocabulary: "This is a door," he would say, and she would repeat "door." He helped her develop social skills: "It's my turn to feed the baby," and then a few seconds later, "Now it's your turn." He helped to develop her imagination: "Look at that cute baby monster," he said as he pointed into an empty cardboard box. I also observed him helping her learn about cause and effect relationships: "If you drop the baby, she will cry"; small- and large-muscle skills: as they fed babies and climbed over chairs to return the baby monster to its home; premath skills: one-to-one correspondence while setting the table; nurturing: he let her cover him with blankets and tuck him into bed; and emotional understanding: "Let's be scared," "Now we have to be brave," "Do you love this baby monster?" Their rich interactions helped both of them deepen their understanding of the world.

In these stories, Siddha and Marygrace were learning several things all at once, without separating them into categories. Adult brains prefer to compartmentalize learning. With that in mind, we will look at how to promote early learning in each of these six categories:

- language and literacy
- math and logical thinking
- science and problem solving
- creative expression and thinking
- social skills and relationships
- physical skills

Language and Literacy

Figuring out language is tough, but baby brains come prepared. From their earliest days, they are listening and using context to apply meaning. Babies are wired to learn the language(s) they are exposed to during their early years. It's not easy. Many words sound alike, and figuring out what they mean, how to use them, and what order to use them in takes practice. Mistakes are made. Here are some examples.

- Marygrace gave a heartfelt "Thank *me!*" instead of "thank you" to show appreciation.
- Hunter liked eating "corn on the cop" when he was little.
- Libby often asked friends to play "tug-a-whore."
- Ty sang "the itchy-bitchy spider."
- Noah watched out the window for trucks and excitedly said, "*Truck!*" when one would drive by. The problem was that he pronounced *truck* with an *f* sound instead of a *tr* sound.

They may fumble around a bit now and then, but infants and toddlers are much more capable when it comes to understanding, comprehending, and learning to use language like a native than we adults. It is worth the effort for them too. I remember when Kada was a little under two. She went to the kitchen, found her bib, put it on, sat at the table, and said, "Me eat now!" It was not mealtime, but what could we do? We fed her. She went to the trouble of learning to say, "Me eat now," so at the very least she earned some crackers and juice. Language is power.

Here are some tips for promoting language development with infants and toddlers:

- Respond to clues and cues.

- Talk a lot.

- Answer questions.

- Use rich and real language.

- Mimic their babble.

- Sing, sing a song.

- Make books available from birth.

- Read and tell stories.

- Let children see you reading.

Respond to Clues and Cues

In chapter 3, I talked about how I messed up with Lilly because I was not paying attention to her clues and cues. My mind was in "I'm an expert" mode instead of "focus on the child" mode. Watching for their clues and cues and responding appropriately are such critical parts of infant and toddler care that we are going to touch on them again here. In the previous chapter, I talked about how important it is to watch for their clues and cues. It is equally important to respond to those clues and cues with what the child needs in that particular moment.

It is important to respond to the clues and cues children give you from the very beginning because this exchange of information is a foundation for the give-and-take of communication. In fact, it is the beginning of communication. Reliably responding to the clues and cues of their facial expressions, body language, verbalizations, and eye contact lets them know their efforts to communicate are effective. Decoding these clues and cues is not always easy (it's hard to tell a real infant smile from the joy of freshly passed gas), but with time, adults can learn to understand their efforts to exchange information. Engaged infants eagerly make eye contact and respond to stimulation, while overstimulated or tired babies tend to turn away from all the action. The best way to tune in to specific infants' clues and cues is to spend focused time getting to know them. Our responsiveness encourages them to keep up the efforts to communicate. Baby Emma has been in our care for about a month. Every day we spend together, I get better at reading her signals. I can even tell when she is smiling and when she is gassy.

Talk a Lot

Infants and toddlers learn words and, more importantly, their meanings, through contextual experience. This means that the more they hear language used, the more of it they are able to understand. Random words printed on flash cards or blurted out by an electronic teddy bear do not have the rich contextual value of words spoken by real people in real conversation. Children decode the meaning of words when they hear them repeatedly in real conversation. For example, two focal points in our child care space are a ninety-gallon aquarium full of fish and another smaller aquarium that houses a turtle. Since the older children spend a lot of time observing and discussing these creatures, the younger ones notice certain words quickly: *fish, water, bubbles, turtle,*

rocks, swim, food, and *eat.* They hear these words a lot, which helps them learn to say them and understand what they mean. Infants and toddlers are constantly monitoring our use of language, and the more they hear, the more they will learn.

Answer Questions

One way to bring more language into the lives of infants and toddlers is to take time to answer their questions. You can even do this with infants who might seem too young—you just have to be tuned in enough to see the questions in their eyes and faces. Responding to their curious and questioning looks empowers them and adds to the day's conversation. You can also make an effort to ask and answer your own questions about things they may be curious about. This takes practice, but it is easier than it might sound.

Answering their questions becomes easier once they can actually verbalize the questions, but easier does not make it easy. How many times can you be asked "Why?" in a single day without your head imploding?

Here is a conversation I overheard years ago between my daughter Zoë, who was about twelve years old and Maddie, who was somewhere between two and three at the time. They were cuddled together reading a book about a pig rolling in mud.

"Why is it rolling in mud, Zoë?"

"Because it wants to cool off. Pigs don't have sweat glands."

"Why, Zoë?"

"Because they don't."

"Why, Zoë?"

"Because that is the way they evolved."

"Why, Zoë?"

"Because they did not need sweat glands, because they had mud to roll in."

"Why, Zoë?"

"Look, can I finish reading the book and then take questions?"

"Okay, Zoë . . . why?"

Throughout this scene, the two made frequent eye contact, snuggled, and read each other's facial expressions. They performed a conversational dance that incorporated their whole bodies. Maddie's eyes lasered questions into Zoë. Zoë deflected them with exaggerated eye rolls. Maddie held Zoë's cheeks in her tiny hands as she asked "Why?" Zoë repeated the gesture with her answers. They repeated this dance, frequently and theatrically.

Here is another conversation I had with Brooke, who was nearly three at the time. Our dance was a little more awkward. I was holding her as we walked through the kitchen.

"What's that, Jeff?"

"That's the refrigerator."

"No, not that. . . . That." Brooke refined her point to a cluster of magnets on the refrigerator door.

"Oh, those are magnets."

"No, not magnets. . . . *That*," she said with an obvious look of frustration.

"What?" I asked with confusion and the same frustration in my eyes.

"*That!* What's . . . that . . . cat?" She spoke slowly, hoping it would help me understand, and pointed at a specific refrigerator magnet.

"Oh, *that*. That's a cat," I said, relieved that this conversation was nearing its conclusion.

"Yep, that's a cat!" she said happily as she gave me a hug. "Why?"

All the questions that pop into children's busy minds and out of their mouths can become annoying and drain our energy, but they are powerful tools for acquiring language and information about the world's workings.

This is where electronic toys, television programs, flash cards, and other materials that claim to help children develop their language skills fail. They are not responsive to the intricate and detailed signals small children send with their questions, expressions, and other clues and cues. Now, the computerized robot teddy bears are going to get smarter and smarter, but they will never be as responsive as an emotionally close and tuned-in human caregiver. Televisions, computer screens, and robot teddy bears are not capable of the reciprocal eye contact and physical closeness that human conversation and interaction provide. The purpose of written and spoken language is to share important information with other human beings. The easiest and most efficient way for small children to do this is to interact naturally with real people. The "learning" gizmos may one day be able to mimic these interactions closely using complex software and motion sensors, but do we really want children looking into the cold life-less eyes of a robotic toy when they ask, "Why?"

Use Rich and Real Language

Not only is it important to talk a lot around infants and toddlers, but it is also important to use rich and real language. The words we use around them should be expressive and vivid. We should make a consistent effort to describe people, places, things, activities, and observations expressively and in detail. The use of rich and real language provides more context, more vocabulary, and more opportunity to hear and absorb the intricacies of verbal communication.

They need to hear words pronounced often and correctly. As we discussed earlier, repetition is important in building neural networks—infants and toddlers need to hear the words they will eventually be able to use over and over again to learn them. The more diverse and varied the language they hear in their early years, the bigger their working vocabularies will become. Knowing more words means having more tools to learn about the world.

Mimic Their Babble

Infants usually start babbling and vocalizing more often between four and six months of age. Mimicking their vocalizations is the beginning of conversation. Not only can your repetition of their sounds and patterns encourage more vocalization, it helps them learn the give and take of conversation. Babbling is talking practice. Mastering the muscle and breath control needed to form the individual sounds that make up a language is a lot of work. All the "babababababamamamambamamaba" and "dada-damabadabadabamaba" is part of the language acquisition process and should be encouraged.

Sing, Sing a Song

Have you ever noticed how adults and older children talk to infants in rhythmic, lilting, singsongy voices? It is almost as if we innately understand that these vocalizations promote language development. The rhythms, patterns, and repetition of music make singing a valuable language development tool. Small children should not only be exposed to recorded music, they should have ample opportunities to hear live music and to sing. Toddlers love to sing—even if they can barely talk. Siddha crawled into my lap recently and said "Rock-a-bye" with a big grin. I wrapped my arms around her long, two-year-old body like she was a little baby and rocked her as I sang the song she requested. She sang along, using words here and there, but mostly mimicking the song's tune. By the time we made it through the song, Annie and Brenden were waiting in line for their turns. I sang the song fifteen times, five times for each of them, before they were ready to move on to other things.

Do you remember how they are learning several things at once? Well, singing not only helps build language skills, but it helps with early math skills too. The patterns of music help children become adept at finding patterns elsewhere, and the rhythms help in their understanding of one-to-one relationships.

You do not have to know a lot of songs or be a great singer to use song as a language-learning tool. You just need to make the effort. I sing about as well as I dance, but my skills are up to the job. Singing with infants and toddlers is not like singing in front of Simon, Randy, Paula, and Kara on *American Idol*. You'll do just fine; give it a try.

Make Books Available from Birth

Infants and toddlers need access to books from their very earliest days. Simply handling books helps them develop the prereading skills that are a necessary foundation for later literacy. Seeing print and associated images is part of the language acquisition process. Early contact with books helps young children learn the difference between positive and negative space on the printed page. (This is simply the ability to differentiate between the foreground—the print or the image—and the background of a page—the white space around the print or the image.) They also begin to learn reading and book etiquette: which way is up, how to turn pages, reading from left to right and top to bottom, and treating books with respect. One day at our house, a toddler accidentally stepped on a stack of books three-year-old Maddie was reading. She looked at the oblivious child and scolded, "We *don't* step on books! We *don't* step on *books!*" At three she was already well aware of the respect and kindness books deserve. If we expect small children to develop into lifelong readers, we must assure that they have regular, easy access to books throughout infancy and toddlerhood.

This does not happen nearly enough, because most books are fragile, and most infants and toddlers are rough on fragile things. Small children are biologically predisposed to learning about the world by tasting it; this makes them the natural enemy of paper. Add to that their innate drive to pull, twist, bend, rip, squeeze, pick, and poke at things, and most ordinary books do not stand a chance. This unintentional roughness leads too many adults to keep books completely out of young children's reach.

Good books are expensive, and it makes sense to want to protect them and make them last, but infants and toddlers need regular and easy access to books. These statements may seem contradictory, but it's possible to find balance. First, widen your definition of what a book is: for infants and toddlers, we are going to consider anything with pictures or words a book. Second, look for options other than standard books with paper pages. Here are some ways to expose infants and toddlers to books without having your books destroyed:

Purchase or make baby-safe cloth books. These fabric books are tough and resilient.

Purchase board books. These books are made from heavy cardboard and will stand up to curious kids. Known in the publishing industry as "chewables," they are designed to hold up to busy baby mouths.

Use environmental print. This refers to the print that appears throughout the child's environment. Cereal, cracker, and other cardboard boxes, as well as plastic food containers, are great options because they are not expensive, they are readily available, they are durable, and they are disposable. Catalogs and newspapers are other environmental print options.

Visit your local public library. The cost is right, and there is no simpler way to expose a child to a wide range of topics and writing styles. The librarian will eagerly help find your favorites and introduce you to new authors.

Children who do not have opportunities for book play, exploration, and discovery in their earliest years are at a disadvantage compared to those who do have that access. A kindergartner who has had books in her hands since birth is far more ready to read than a classmate who has not.

Read and Tell Stories

Of course, the best way to expose small children to books is to let them help you hold the book and turn pages while sitting in your lap during story time. This gives them a chance to observe the intricacies of reading and see how the professional does the job. Hearing you read is like up-close, on-the-job reading training. Children who are read to become readers. It is amazing to watch. For example, in our child care program, six-year-old Katie spent the summer after kindergarten reading to Brooke. This gave her an opportunity to improve her reading skills and share those skills with Brooke, who had just turned four. This was a wonderful opportunity for Brooke. Our house became a reading oasis in a life that otherwise lacked books and reading. She made dramatic improvement in her prereading skills and her desire to read. Then, as soon as Katie went back to school in the fall, I noticed Brooke sitting by the bookshelf "reading" to three-year-old Maddie. It is no wonder that from the time she was two-and-a-half, Maddie's favorite question to adults and older children has been "Hey, want to read books?" The cycle continues: children who are read to read.

But reading is not your only option. Telling stories, whether you have memorized them or make them up on the spot, is another way to share rich language with children. Their little minds are biologically predisposed to listen to stories. Here are some tips for storytelling:

Relax and have fun. You do not have to spin tales like the Brothers Grimm or Mark Twain to be a successful storyteller. Just relax and enjoy the story yourself. If you can do this, the child is bound to enjoy the story.

Be descriptive. Make use of your vocabulary and take the time to add detail to the scenes you create. Paint pictures with words that the child will see clearly.

Practice. Becoming comfortable telling stories takes practice. You might want to start with *Goldilocks and the Three Bears*, *The Three Little Pigs*, or another very familiar and favorite story from your own childhood to build your confidence before heading out into the unknown of your own imagination.

Rely on reality. Sharing memories of real events may be more powerful than sharing stories of make-believe, because it draws the listening children into the world of the teller—into your world.

Add the child to the story. Children love to become characters in stories, especially when they get to be the hero or have an adventure.

Let them help. Pause every once in a while and ask for suggestions about what should happen next, and then build those suggestions into the story.

Let them predict. It is also good to stop periodically and let the child guess what will happen next. Making predictions is a big part of learning to read and understanding conversations, and story time is a safe place to practice this skill.

Repeat Yourself. Repetition is a big part of storytelling. Look at any collection of quality children's books, and you will find repetitive sounds, phrases, and structure. These things bind stories together and help children make predictions about what is coming next. The repetition is often the most memorable part of the story. Which books do these lines come from?

"I'll huff and I'll puff!"

"I do not like them, Sam I Am!"

"Time for bed, Biscuit."

". . . What do you see?"

Children not only love repetition in stories, they love repetition of stories. You'll find you do not need to invent a new story every day; they will want to hear previous stories over and over and over again.

Let Children See You Reading

You are a professional role model, and the young children in your care are your apprentices. They learn from observing you. It is vital that they see you reading on a regular basis. Reading to them is important, but they need to see more. They have to see you reading for your own enjoyment and edification. Seeing adults reading regularly, seeing reading as a tool to better know the world, seeing it as a source of enjoyment, seeing it as something adults do—all have an important impact on the wiring of those busy, bendy little brains.

Hunter and Maddie were best friends while they were in our care. He was a year older than she was. Sometimes I think she learned to speak just so she could talk his ear off. She was constantly chattering at him as they ate, built with blocks, colored, ran around outside, settled down for rest time, played house, read books, sang songs, and put on their shoes. One day when Maddie was nearly three, Hunter said, "Maddie, you talk too much. Can we have a little quiet time?"

When it comes to talking and reading, "too much" is almost impossible. We need to immerse infants and toddlers in written and spoken language so it becomes an expected and natural part of their daily experience. We must choose quality person-to-person communications over electronic media and other supposed "learning" toys because the face-to-face interactions are richer. Language is about communicating with other people. It requires a give-and-take exchange of information, reciprocal eye contact and other forms of body language, and focused attention, which are learned best through human interaction.

This interaction must begin early, because language acquisition starts in the earliest days of life. Infants know a lot of language before they can actually speak. Before Annie had words, she would randomly drop what she was doing and run to me with a smile. I would pick her up and ask, "Where is my hug?" All smiles and twinkling eyes, she would pull her torso away from me and shrug her shoulders. I would ask again, "Where is my hug?" Her arms stiffened against her sides and she turned her head away. She watched me out of the corners of her dancing eyes. I'd ask one more time. After a dramatic pause, she would finally lunge at me, wrap her arms around my neck, and nuzzle her head into my shoulder. We carried on many conversations before she said her first words; we have been practicing and refining our skills since she was a few weeks old. Infants and toddlers crave conversation, they yearn for words, they turn toward voices, they bounce to songs, and they babble to baby dolls. They are born to communicate. Our job is to assure that their play, exploration, and discovery of the world is full of regular and rich language opportunities.

Math and Logical Thinking

Every once in a while, four-wheel-drive Brenden's busy legs come to a complete stop for a moment or two. When he is not plowing through hedges or trying to walk off chairs, he likes to sit and line up blocks. His nimbler-by-the-day fingers slowly arrange one block after another in rows three- or four-feet long. Frequently, he accidentally nudges one out of place with a wayward hand or foot and pauses to correct the error carefully. Then he continues work on his block line, his little tongue protruding from his mouth in concentration. Sometimes it is not a line of blocks; it is a line of cars. Once, it was molded plastic animals: a lion, followed by a pig, followed by a cow and calf, followed by an alligator, followed by a chicken.

It is amazing to see a body that is almost in constant motion sit still for so long and work so carefully. He used to walk right through block rows and towers other children had built, like Godzilla flattening Tokyo. For a while, I wondered if he noticed anything in his path, but now I realize his rush from place to place did not diminish his observational skills in the least. He watched the older children stack blocks and line up cars. Then he started doing what he had seen them model.

When it is time to put all the blocks and cars and plastic animals away, he does his best to put things where they go, just like he has seen the big kids do. His attention wanders a bit when there is a big mess, but he seems to enjoy helping restore order to the chaotic playroom. The modeling does not stop there. Brenden heads to the kitchen at mealtime to get his cup and bring it to his highchair. This is something he started almost as soon as he could walk, because he had been watching older children do this since he was tiny.

All of this is the beginning of his understanding of mathematics and logical thinking. It is a long way from calculus. Heck, it is a long way from $2 + 2 = 4$—but it is his first steps toward both those things. Through all this play, exploration, and discovery, Brenden is classifying the universe, sorting out the world, seeing similarities and differences in the things he encounters, creating patterns, understanding one-to-one correspondence, learning about "If . . . then" relationships, and many other things that lay the foundation for formal learning about math and logical thinking.

Math and logical thinking for infants and toddlers is not about numbers, equations, solving for x, theorems, variables, remainders, carrying the 2, deductive or inductive reasoning, sound or unsound arguments, finding the mean, or fallacies. Math and logical thinking for infants and toddlers are about playing, exploring, and discovering. They are not about abstractions; they are about interacting with a stable and predictable universe. They are about stacking blocks, finding your cup, and putting the plastic cow on the right shelf when it is time for lunch.

Helping infants and toddlers make these small leaps in their understanding of math and logical thinking does not happen with flash cards, worksheets, number lines, computers, electronic toys, or "educational" television and DVDs. Learning to say "1, 2, 3, 4, 5, 6, 7, 8, 9, 10 . . ." or "2 + 3 = 5" is not learning math. It is learning words.

Learning math and logical thinking requires interaction with the physical world so that there is meaning behind those words. It happens by providing safe emotional environments, rich physical environments, and time to play, explore, and discover. Children need to line up a lot of blocks and cars to realize that adding new items always makes the line longer and taking them away always makes the line shorter. *Always.* They need to put many toys away to realize that certain things always belong with certain other things because they share characteristics. *Always.* They need to try walking off a lot of chairs before realizing that *if* they try to walk off a chair, *then* they will fall. *Always.* They need to spend a lot of time fiddling with puzzle pieces before they begin seeing how those pieces always fit together the same way. *Always.* Math and logical thinking are about *always.* Young children need experiences that lead to certainty before they can move to abstractions. The early years are about gaining that certainty in preparation for later learning.

Here are some suggestions for helping small children gain the certainty they need about the universe:

- Make available a wide selection of manipulatives (blocks, cars, empty containers, stones, sticks, cardboard tubes).

- Provide age-appropriate puzzles (one to five pieces).

- Talk about shapes, sizes, and relationships of things (big/small, in/out, over/under) while children interact with the manipulatives.

- Let them see you or other children stacking, arranging, sorting, and classifying the materials.

• Allow plenty of time for them to interact with the materials on their own.

This basic foundation will lead to counting, then to addition and subtraction, then to more advanced ciphering, and then to more advanced, abstract thinking. There is no need to hurry this or push it to happen. It happens quickly enough. The other day, Siddha was paging through an old copy of *National Geographic* when she spied a picture of a snake. With wide eyes she shouted, "'Nake," and dropped the magazine in my lap. Then she went on a scavenger hunt. One by one, she brought me a "snake" made out of green milk jug lids strung together, a molded plastic snake, and three books—all turned to pages with pictures of snakes. Then she noticed a turtle in one of the three books and carried it across the room to show the real turtle sunning himself in his tank—stopping to pick up another molded plastic turtle along the way.

She has been busy sorting and classifying the world over the last two years. She understands with certainty what makes a snake a snake, what makes a turtle a turtle, and so much more. She is well on her way to advanced math and logic, but for now it's time to pick up the toys.

Science and Problem Solving

There is little difference between early math and logical thinking and early science and problem solving. Everything in the previous section fits snugly under the science and problem-solving banner. The language section could fit under this heading too. Small children learn language through problem solving and experimentation. *Everything* infants and toddlers do is science. Hunter pooping on his hand was science. Siddha putting the ring around her ankles and walking was science. Annie not biting was science. Lilly watching the older children play was science, and Brenden picking pine-cones was science. All the touching, tasting, observing, smelling, and listening is science. All of their often-awkward interactions with people and objects are science. Human babies are born scientists; all they do from the time they wake to the time they drift off to sleep is science. They are born biologically wired for learning about the world through scientific inquiry.

Granted, their methods are not as rigorous, thoughtful, and planned as those of adult scientists. Infants and toddlers are so new to their bodies and the world that their experiments often look crude, awkward, and simplistic. I have never heard of anyone winning a Nobel Prize, receiving a huge research grant, or changing our understanding of how the world works by pooping on his or her own hand, but I would wager that most of history's greatest scientists performed similarly icky experiments as part of their earliest research. All of us start life as scientists, but most of us end up doing other things for a living.

The word *science* comes from the Latin word *scientia* and means "to know." Human babies have been actively doing science, trying "to know," much longer than the word *science* has been around. Most of their scientific inquiry revolves around understanding four things:

- their bodies

- relationships

- language

- physical reality

Bodies

Much of children's first three years is spent learning efficient and effective use of their bodies. From grasping objects, coordinating movements, and rolling over to walking, jumping, and regulating their bladders and bowels, they need time to master their marvelous human bodies. Each new skill is a tool useful in further experimentation and deeper understanding of the world. Grasping allows contact with nearby objects, hand-eye coordination allows for better manipulation of available objects, and locomotion makes it possible to go way over there to check out different objects and get to know them. Understanding their bodies makes it easier for children to understand the world.

Relationships

Interactions with other people are important from the very beginning. Not only do infants and toddlers rely on us for their safety and well-being, they depend on us to help them know the world. These first relationships are the foundation for all future relationships. This is why it is so important that we are clearheaded, focused, and ready to dance. They are learning about nurturing, empathy, dependability, trust, respect, and unconditional love through their early interactions with other people—or at least they should be. Too many small children learn the exact opposite of these things in their early relationships, and doing so sets the pattern for their adult years. Not having experienced unconditional love, dependability, and respect as toddlers makes it hard for many adults to experience or recognize those things.

Unconditional love and all the rest are not always easy to give when children are stuffing cereal up their nose and riding laundry baskets down the stairs. The reason the twos seem so terrible to some caregivers is that at this age children perform many relationship experiments. They try out the word *no*, find and push our buttons, exert some independence, and try to see just how far they can go.

Adults can support children's learning by thinking of ourselves as good lab assistants while children are doing relationship science (or any other learning). The world is their laboratory and they are *always* experimenting, trying to figure out the complexities of being human. When it comes to relationships, they experiment with different personas, actions, and reactions, trying out new ways of interacting with the world. Then they watch how the world reacts. They are *always* watching the way others act and react. As good lab assistants, we must anticipate their needs, respond appropriately and consistently to their experiments, and model the relationship dynamics we want them eventually to internalize. I want the children in my life to use their words, be respectful, think before acting, and consider the feelings of others. This means that I am always trying to model these behaviors and have high expectations for the children. It also means that I am willing to apologize when I mess up and forgive when they mess up. Relationship science is another tool for knowing the world and interpersonal problem solving. When you learn to interact with other people effectively, you also gain a valuable and trusted source for other knowledge about the world.

Language

The acquisition of language takes a lot of experimentation and requires the development of physical as well as mental skills. Children experiment with vocalizations, word use and syntax, and the formation of letters. This experimentation is done best in the real world through real human-to-human interaction. (Videos, computers, talking robot teddy bears, and flash cards all lack the intricate give and take of real, person-to-person communication.) As a lab assistant helping children discover language, your job is to introduce new words, model good language skills, and engage them in lots and lots of conversation. We learn language by using language.

To do this, we need to use language correctly. It is great when a fourteen-month-old asks for "wa wa"—that is a marvelous step toward the word *water*. What is not so great is when the whole family starts calling water "wa wa." This makes it difficult for the child to learn to say the word correctly. (Have no fear—they will catch on by second or third grade, after they have spent time with people who say "water.") At the other extreme, there are the adults who correct every verbal misstep a child makes from the first time she says, "Mama." "No, Jennifer, the word is *mo-ther*, not Mama. Say *mo-ther*." We do not need to dumb language down for children, and we do not need to correct their mistakes. We just need to expose them to plenty of language. The best thing you can do as a lab assistant is keep the communication flowing.

Children's experiments get the job done; language quickly becomes a powerful tool that leads to new experiences and learning opportunities.

The power of questions such as "Why?" and "What's that?" opens up completely new worlds to young children. Using words makes new activities, skills, and interactions possible. It also makes solving problems easier. One of the first phrases children in our care learn is "Help me." They know that these words will bring assistance when they become frustrated while doing something for themselves. Using words also improves their vocabularies— providing even more tools for knowing the world and solving problems.

Physical Reality

Much of early science involves getting to know the physical world and how its assorted bits and pieces interact. Infanthood and toddlerhood are full of discoveries: the sound of ripping paper; the smell, taste, and texture of wet sand; the subtle variations of green on a grasshopper's back; the sight and sound of bubbles blown in a glass of cold milk with a twisty straw; the smell of Mommy's neck after a shower; the sight of dancing dust particles in a beam of late summer sunshine; the feel and smell of fresh pajamas after a bath; the whirl of activity after milk is spilled; the texture and taste of a rock-hard french fry pulled from the car seat; the sound of wind whispering in willow trees. Children eagerly discover these things and every other little bit of daily life we take for granted in our busy adult lives.

Even the earliest months of life are full of problems to start solving:

- Why does this thing they put in my hand make rattling sounds when I move my arm?

- How can I get the rattling thing back after I drop it?

- Why doesn't the rattling thing fall to the ceiling when I drop it?

- Does the rattling thing *ever* fall to the ceiling?

- Why doesn't my tummy feel full after sucking on the rattling thing?

- Who took my rattling thing?

- Does the rattling thing exist if I can't see it?

- How come I can rip the crinkly stuff but I can't rip the rattling thing?

Their bendy baby minds don't have the capacity to think about these problems in words or any other way we fully understand, but their consistent exploration and discoveries eventually lead to answers. In general, their efforts to understand the physical world revolve around understanding three things:

- the properties of objects (color, texture, taste, smell, shape, etc.)
- how objects interact (cause-and-effect relationships)
- what makes objects similar and different (classification)

Most infants and toddlers go about knowing the universe unobtrusively. To the casual observer, all this discovery and problem solving might look like a bunch of nothing. Sometimes we have to look closely to see it happening. I watched one winter morning as one-year-old Marygrace placed her ear to the refrigerator door and smiled at the gentle hum in her head. Then she turned and tried the other ear and smiled the same happy smile. Next, she moved to a cabinet door, trying one ear and then the other—no hum, no smile. After a few more cabinets, she came to the dishwasher. After she placed her ear to its door, her little feet danced and her face lit up as she listened to the whir and splash of water. I joined her, and we shared a smile.

Later that day, I watched as she joined Siddha and Annie in dragging toddler chairs across the playroom to the window. They climbed onto their chairs and watched the snow. Then, realizing the glass was cold, they took turns touching it, making surprised faces, and giggling. After a few minutes of this, they moved on to licking the cold pane of glass. They were gleeful at the new sensation. I let them fully enjoy their discovery before washing the window. Then I gave it a lick to see if it was really worth all the excitement. Maybe I should have done this before cleaning the window. All I experienced was a tongueful of glass cleaner.

Creative Expression and Thinking

Early math, science, and thinking skills generally focus on gaining understanding of the physical world. The never-ending play, exploration, and discovery build an ever-growing database of information about the interrelation of worldly objects. All of this leads to a firmer understanding of the real world and prepares young minds for symbolic reasoning, which most children acquire somewhere around thirty months of age. All brains develop differently; some children start using symbols earlier and some later. According to John Medina, author of *Brain Rules* (2008), "Exhaustive studies show that symbolic reasoning, this all-important human trait, takes almost three years of experience to become fully operational. We don't appear to do much to distinguish ourselves from apes before we are out of the terrible twos" (33–34). For infants and young toddlers, a block is a block. It is only a block, and they do not picture it as anything other than a block. They are content to explore the object as it is, coming to know its intrinsic blockiness.

When children develop symbolic reasoning, which is the ability to use one thing to represent something else, a completely new world opens. What once was just a block now becomes a symbol for a host of other things: a car, a cell phone, a piece of pie, a glass of milk, a baby doll bottle, an airplane, a cow, a book, a butterfly, a credit card, a gun, a wrench or harmonica, a laser sword, a spider, a stapler, a pen, or anything else a bendy little mind can imagine. With symbolic reasoning, what once was just a block structure becomes a house, a dinosaur cage, an office building, a shed, a zoo, a giraffe, a plate of scrambled eggs, a city, an airport, or an interstate highway system. Plastic two-part hair curlers become bowls of cereal, candles, or hot dogs and buns. A cardboard box comes to represent a dog kennel, a fire engine, a cave that is home to an angry monster, a clubhouse, or a baby bed. Sometimes the same box will be six things in ten minutes. Sometimes identical blocks will serve as cars, airplanes, roads, houses, people, and buildings in the same play scenario. Then again, sometimes they are just boxes and blocks.

Push the pause button on your life for a moment and think about how utterly amazing it is that our babies possess brains capable of doing this at all, let alone before blowing out the candles on their third birthday cake. This ability leads to spoken and then written language, mathematics, engineering, books, art, music, computers—every piece of our human civilization is related to symbolic reasoning.

Many "educational" toys actually hinder the development of symbolic thinking and creativity. The link to the licensed characters that adorn many of these toys is so strong that it is hard for children to separate the toy from the character. Too often I have seen children scold other kids who are playing with licensed character dolls or action figures that they are doing it "wrong" because that is not the way it is done on the TV show or in the movie. Children buy into the characters' personas so strongly that it affects their ability to imagine new and creative play scenarios. These items clutter the play environment and limit imagination. The electronic gizmos, many of them also tied to licensed characters, are not any better. Cardboard boxes or blank paper and crayons do more to promote creativity than a fuzzy robot teddy bear or a talking "pretend" computer. Children get bored with the fancy gear very quickly because it is so one-dimensional. I know parents and caregivers who have closets, basements, garages, and storage units full of these "learning" toys that kids quickly toss aside in favor of other play materials.

Promote real creativity in your physical play environment in these ways:

- Shut off the television and computer.
- Get rid of licensed character action figures and dolls.
- Toss out all the flashing, winking, and blinking electronic gizmos.
- Provide chunks of time for child-directed play, exploration, and discovery.
- Make sure playtime with the above materials is uninterrupted and safe.
- Listen to a variety of recorded and live music.
- Tell stories.
- Offer open-ended and flexible play materials.

Not sure what will keep children engaged, or what open-ended and flexible means? An open-ended material is something that can easily be used in more than one way, something that lends itself to a child's creativity and use of symbolic reasoning. Try some of these materials:

- cardboard boxes
- blank paper and markers, pens, pencils, and crayons
- sand, dirt, and water
- various dress-up clothes and dramatic play props
- homemade musical instruments
- assorted paints and applicators
- blocks, blocks, and more blocks

When you combine a supportive emotional environment with open-ended materials and ample playtime, creativity will happen. It is in our DNA. Our human brains are biologically wired to adapt and think creatively. This is not something we have to push on children. We simply need to set the stage and allow them to practice thinking and expressing themselves in new ways. Look back at our history, and you will find that creative people were not made creative but allowed to be creative. In moments of flow, they combined bits of prior knowledge and experience in unique ways to create something new. The best thing you can do is set the stage and allow creativity to happen.

Doing this means they may not use the materials the way you had intended or expected; they may not use things the way you consider to be right. This is okay; in fact, this is real creativity. It's often hard for adults who were not allowed this freedom as children to relax and let creative play/ learning happen. We have to be willing to give up some of our control— maybe it is okay to draw on the wooden blocks with markers, paint with your toes, haul infants and toddlers out into a spring rain, mix shredded paper and water in the sensory table, or make circles out of green beans.

Social Skills and Relationships

Much of what infants and toddlers learn about social skills and relationships is through experiences and interactions with you, their caregiver. As a professional role model, you must always be aware that they are constantly watching and will model what they see, hear, and experience. If you look, you will see examples of this in their behavior.

- Siddha pretending to water plants with an empty yogurt container after seeing Tasha water them for real.

- Maddie telling toddlers not to step on books after hearing those words many times before.

- Brenden running to the kitchen to get his sippy cup for lunch.

- Marygrace sitting next to me, feeding a doll while I feed baby Lilly.

Small children who observe and experience good social skills and strong relationships will develop the skills, the neural connections, to make those things a part of their lives. They learn kindness and unconditional love by experiencing kindness and unconditional love. Marygrace, Siddha, and Annie spent most of their first two years together in our care. I knew our program's emotional environment was working when they all started walking. Their new mobility meant opportunities for a broader range of experiences. They could get to new toys, interact more fully with older children, and physically put themselves into fresh situations. This provided them with new learning opportunities, but the newness of it all also meant more hurt feelings, frustration, and tears.

What we quickly found was that the three of them were there for each other. If Siddha crashed off a chair on the other side of the room, Marygrace and Annie would rush to hug her and pat her on the head. If Annie became frustrated with the stacking cups, Siddha would toddle up with her favorite doll. These three had been physically close and emotionally tuned in to each other—and to me and Tasha—since infancy. Their ability to empathize, calm, and comfort each other was amazing. They still had disputes and disagreements, but overall, their strong bonds made this often-tense part of toddlerhood smooth.

You can support the natural development of social skills and relationships in these ways:

- Respond to clues and cues.

- Provide opportunity for interaction.

- Give responsibility.

- Nurture relationships.

- Support dramatic play.

Respond to Clues and Cues

Professional role modeling with infants and toddlers revolves around responsive care, and this means tuning in to their clues and cues. We've talked about clues and cues before, but now we are going to look at how this responsiveness helps develop social skills and build relationships. Here's an example of how it works:

The other day Brenden, age two, was attempting to build a wall around three toy cars. He had watched the older boys building shops and garages for their cars and was attempting to make one of his own. It was not working. His fine-motor skills are amazing, but they were not up to the task at this moment. He was tired, it was almost lunchtime, and every once in a while, a pea green snoterpillar crawled from his left nostril. With a frustrated swipe of his arm, he swept the cars and blocks onto the floor. Then he pushed Annie as he stormed away from the table. Expecting him to pick up the blocks or make nice with Annie would have been too much. We were doing the I'm-tired-I'm-hungry-and-I-don't-feel-too-good-hustle. I responded to his cues appropriately. I fed him, wiped his nose, and let him take a nap. When he woke up a few hours later, he built a garage for his cars.

When we tune in to children—dancing that early childhood cha-cha—our relationships grow stronger. As they grow, they will use those early relationships as models for future relationships. Responding appropriately to their needs as infants and toddlers helps them learn to expect similar responses throughout their lives.

Provide Opportunity for Interaction

Learning about relationships, like learning about language, science, and math, requires practice and repetition. Developing social skills and learning how to be part of an interpersonal relationship means practicing those things. Young children need many opportunities to interact with a variety of people in a variety of situations. This is how they practice, how they get the needed repetition. Marygrace, Siddha, and Annie related so well with each other because they had had plenty of practice.

We can help small children practice interacting by providing plenty of face-to-face time for those interactions to take place. From their earliest days, infants should get out of the solitary confinement of cribs and swings and look at, reach for, and touch other babies. Toddlers need time to tickle each other's toes, find their buddy's nose, examine physical differences, and get to know each other. This might lead to disagreements, but there is nothing wrong with that. The only way to learn to handle disagreements effectively is to experience disagreements. You learn that your friend does not like to have her hair pulled by pulling her hair. You learn that biting hurts by being bit. (Although some misguided adults still think it is okay to bite toddlers to teach them a lesson, being bit *does not* teach you not to bite.) You learn about sharing by sharing, you learn about taking turns by taking turns, and you learn about using your words by using your words. All of this is part of the learning process and takes a lot of practice.

Give Responsibility

Efficiently and effectively navigating interpersonal relationships requires personal responsibility. We have to learn that we are responsible for bringing something to every one of our relationships. We have to understand that there is a give-and-take to relationships. People who never learn this plague the world. Some are all take and no give. They live their lives expecting, demanding, and insisting. Then they pout, whine, and complain when things do not go their way. Others are all give and no take. They spend so much time giving to others that they do not know how to accept help, take time for themselves, or see their value as individuals. They blow up, fall apart, resent the world, or quietly implode. Neither of these extremes is healthy. The balance of give *and* take is what we should strive for in our lives and model for the children for whom we care.

Giving toddlers appropriate responsibilities helps them learn they are part of something, that they must give if they want to receive. It helps them become competent and confident in their relationships and in other parts of their lives. If they learn some personal responsibility early in life, they are more apt to be personally responsible as adults.

Watching them be responsible is fun. One-year-old Annie was putting toys away before lunch. She walked across the room with two play plates and a cup in her hands, using her chin to keep them all there. She opened the drawer where they all belonged, put one plate in and closed the drawer; opened it again, put the other plate in and closed the drawer; opened the drawer again, put the cup in, and closed the drawer. Then she smiled with pride at a job well done, pride at being a contributing part of the group.

Nurture Relationships

Nurturing children as individuals and nurturing our unique relationships with each one of them builds strong attachments. These attachments are the foundation for their knowledge about relationships and other learning. When we make them feel safe, secure, and anchored, they are able and willing to go off and form new relationships, have new experiences, and try new things.

One day at the neighborhood park around the corner from my house, Kada, then one and a half, spotted a squirrel sitting on a fence about ten yards away. After glancing at me for approval, she ran toward it with a huge smile. The squirrel chattered and leaped to a mulberry tree trunk. Kada stopped just short of the tree and chattered some toddler chatter at the squirrel, who was now on a branch about eight feet above her head. Now both of them were chattering. In an instant, the squirrel jumped to a lower branch, and Kada ran to my side with fear in her eyes. The squirrel watched. Kada took me by the hand and brought me to the tree, where we sat on the ground and watched as the critter scampered and munched mulberries.

I was her security blanket. The strength of our relationship made her brave enough to approach the squirrel on her own, and she knew she could run to me when the situation became overwhelming. The strength of our relationship, our attachment, also made it easier for her to approach new children at the park. She would run to greet them with the same huge smile and usually ended up chattering with a new friend. When it comes to helping infants and toddlers build strong relationships and social skills, our job is to be their security blanket.

Relationships with children are not the only ones that need nurturing. Our relationships with other adults often do not get the attention they need when we focus so completely on children. There have been times when my relationship with Tasha was hurt by our strong focus on caring for our own and other people's children. We were so busy with these responsibilities that we didn't take the time to nurture our relationship. I see this happen often with parents and child care providers. In 2008, I traveled over 40,000 miles to give presentations and talk with caregivers about stress and burnout. Caregivers feel guilty about taking time to nurture their adult relationships or personal needs. They feel there is not enough time in the day to care for everyone who needs their attention. They get so child focused that they let their adult relationships falter. To be your best for children, you need to invest time in nurturing all your relationships. Make time for a date with your sweetie. Go to dinner with friends. Spend time with your own kids. Invest in the care and maintenance of all your emotional environments.

Support Dramatic Play

Hunter was almost three when he plopped himself down on my lap and said, "It's hard saying, 'Meow, meow, meow,' a lot." He had been busily engaged in a dramatic play scenario in which he was the family cat. He had to meow for his food, meow for a pillow, meow for someone to pet him, meow when he found a mouse, and meow when he wanted a kitty treat. Dramatic play provides many opportunities for young children to practice different social roles, tactics, and personas, although most of them do not become masters at this type of play until after the age of three. Pretend play allows them to fool around at being nice, mean, angry, kind, gentle, obnoxious, rude, belligerent, unruly, wild, meek, evasive, loving, silly, glib, funny, and every other trait they can imagine in a safe setting. It also allows them to work out experiences from their own lives in the same safety. The hustle and bustle of the fast-moving adult world can be overwhelming to young children. Reenacting elements from that adult world in their fantasy play gives them a chance to understand what they see, hear, and experience.

Providing a variety of props and dress-up clothes, along with plenty of child-directed time, is a great way to promote this type of play. If you are invited to join in the play, follow the lead of the child(ren) and avoid casting yourself as the lead character. Do what you can to expand and build on their themes without taking over. Enjoy the dance, but remember to let them lead.

Physical Skills

Before starting to cruise along furniture or take his first steps, baby Ty repeatedly pulled himself up to stand, let go, and fell to his bottom. He was experimenting with his body, getting to know his muscles. Enjoying the sensations, he did this repeatedly in preparation for walking. He was strengthening and gaining control over large muscles in his legs and torso that he would rely on for his whole life.

When Brenden lines up cars or blocks, he is doing more than early math; he is training the small muscles in his hands and wrists to move precisely. Each block he places reinforces and strengthens a connection in his brain, hardwiring the skill into his bendy brain.

As Lilly enjoys time on the floor watching the other children, she passes a toy from one hand to the other. This not only builds her small-muscle skills; it wires brain connections that allow her hands to work in harmony with her eyes. Hardwiring this skill now will allow her to drive her friends to the mall without hitting a tree when she is seventeen.

As with language and the other arbitrary categories we have created here for our adult minds, the development of physical skills begins at the beginning. Infants and toddlers are constantly strengthening their large and small muscles, refining their use, and building the neural connections that control all those muscles and their precise movements.

Where is the best place to develop and hone muscle strength and coordination? An open area of floor will do just fine. What special equipment is necessary to support infants and toddlers in developing these skills? None.

Walkers, bouncy seats, baby gyms, and swings restrain children unnaturally and hinder their biologically driven efforts to build their bodies. These pieces of equipment seemingly make life easier for adults, but too many infants are sentenced to lull themselves to sleep in swings or vibrating bouncy seats instead of rolling around on the floor. Too many of them are confined to flopping around like rag dolls in exersaucers instead of rocking back and forth on their hands and knees. This gear is unnatural and tends to overstimulate babies. The reason they fall asleep in musical swings and vibrating bouncy seats is because their senses become overloaded and their brains turn to sleep as a defense against the excessive stimulation. Some of this gear also puts babies in upright positions before they are physically ready and may cause stress on immature hip joints and pelvises. There is a natural physical progression from infancy to toddlerhood, and this gear is messing with that progression.

I've visited centers where rows of sleeping infants rhythmically rock back and forth in matching swings, lulled to sleep by confinement and overstimulation. Other programs I have visited incarcerate infants and toddlers in individual cribs. The children look dazed and confused—like prisoners confined to their cells. Such practices are wrong. It is not respectful to the infants, and it does nothing to promote their development. Keeping a child content and quiet for eight or ten hours while her parents work is not the same as nurturing that child's growing mind and body. I have heard the phrase "a quiet baby is a happy baby" too often. It is simply not true. A happy baby is an active baby, fully engaged in her environment and treated with respect.

If we really believe that infants and toddlers are capable learners from their earliest days and that they deserve our respect, as Pikler and Gerber suggest, then it makes sense to get rid of the unneeded gear, clear some floor space, and get the babies and ourselves down on the floor for natural, child-centered, and child-driven activity.

Clearing the floor of all the limiting and unnatural gear creates space for materials that really enhance small- and large-muscle development. It will come as no surprise that these are the same materials that lead to other infant and toddler learning. Here is a short and incomplete list:

- cardboard boxes and tubes
- blocks
- books
- paper
- dress-up clothes
- sand and water
- dolls
- dramatic play props
- empty plastic containers (yogurt, butter)
- recorded music

If we clear their environments of unneeded clutter and provide some basic materials that promote child-centered activity, the learning of physical skills will happen. Once we set the stage, our job is to maintain a safe environment and be available to assist in their play, exploration, and discovery.

Brenden and Annie were busy stacking an assortment of cardboard boxes, baby-wipe containers, blocks, and stuffed animals. This play scenario began when I built a structure from these materials that towered over their heads and then allowed them to knock it down. The excitement of the crash captured their attention as much as the sight of the tall tower. As they built, they strengthened their large and small muscles and refined their movement and coordination. They giggled as they tried new materials and arrangements—the beginning of creativity. Each crash reinforced their knowledge of gravity and other principles of the physical world. Each new object made the tower taller, and each one that fell made it smaller—this is toddler math. When the tower began to lean, they tried to hold it up—problem solving and creative thinking. All of this play, exploration, and discovery—all of this learning—took place in a relaxed environment where they were respected and treated like thinkers, an environment where their caregivers were ready and willing to dance.

Early learning is not complicated, but we tend to overcomplicate it. It is not rocket science, but it leads to rocket science.

TAKING CARE OF YOURSELF

Visualization

Getting from where we are in life to where we want to be is a challenging journey. One of the first steps on this journey is to create a clear mental image of where you want go, of what your destination looks like. For example, if you want to become a more thoughtful and tuned-in caregiver, you must intentionally create a lucid and focused mental picture of yourself being more thoughtful and more tuned-in. The following visualization technique is a helpful tool for creating the needed mental images.

1. Sit comfortably with eyes closed.

2. Breathe normally.

3. Allow your mind to settle; acknowledge thoughts that pop into your head, then release them.

4. After a few moments, begin visualizing yourself with the young children for whom you care. Paint a mental picture of yourself being the best caregiver possible. See yourself as you want to be: more focused, more patient, more open, less harsh, less rushed, less judgmental. Imagine the best possible you, the ideal caregiver.

5. Spend time with this image. Add action and dimension to the scene. How do you act and react? What does the setting look like? How do you carry yourself? What is your tone of voice like? What differences are there between your reality and your vision of perfection?

6. When you are ready, slowly return to the real world. It might be handy to have a pen and paper nearby to jot down any insights you may have.

7. Repeat this exercise periodically to hone your vision of yourself as an ideal caregiver.

Visualization is also a useful tool for decision making and problem solving. Use the technique described above to picture the results of the various choices to a given problem. The act of visualizing the different scenarios can bring clarity and enhance your decision-making skills.

Out for Breakfast

T asha and I walked to a restaurant down the street one Sunday morning this summer. While eating breakfast, I watched as two young children giggled and goofed with their parents, grandparents, and other family members at a nearby table. Pleasant conversation flowed as the younglings moved from lap to lap, asking questions, manipulating silverware, tasting waffles and eggs. The toddlers babbled in response to questions from their grandpa, stacked plastic containers of cream and jelly with an older child, and snuggled with Mommy. This is early learning; this is what play, exploration, and discovery look like for infants and toddlers. It is simple, relaxed, unhurried, and dependent upon a strong emotional environment, one that offers safety, freedom, and unconditional love. This was a great example of adults taking control of the small picture. They were actively engaged in focusing and attending to those young children, on nurturing their needs in the moment. There were no handheld video games or robot teddy bears. There were no flash cards or developmentally inappropriate learning games. There was simply a family being together and involving the young children in that togetherness.

We left the restaurant and returned to a beautiful summer morning and the reality that not every child is as fortunate as the two we had observed while eating waffles and eggs. Across the street from the restaurant, we could not help but notice four police officers and their vehicles surrounding two women with strollers in a gas station parking lot. A curious and confused toddler watched from each stroller as the officers and women talked. I wanted to stop and watch, to see what the problem was, to see how this scene unfolded, but we walked on.

Tuesday's newspaper told the story. What was the hubbub and hullabaloo we had witnessed? It seems the two women were operating their strollers erratically. Someone called the police, who stopped, charged, and arrested the women for strolling while intoxicated.

Let it sink in for a moment—strolling . . . while . . . intoxicated.

Strolling down the street while intoxicated on a bright Sunday morning with two beautiful babies. Had they been drinking all night? Had they started drinking early in the morning to get a jump on the day? How frequently did this happen? What else did they expose those beautiful children to? What kind of emotional environment do those babes live in? What are their mommies doing to promote play, exploration, and discovery?

Even sadder than this incident of strolling while intoxicated is the fact that this kind of thing is common. Infants and toddlers are continually caught up in their adult caregivers' dramas, constantly burdened by bad adult choices. This is the big-picture reality of the world we are living in. There seems to be an endless supply of people making thoughtless choices involving young children. There seems to be no end to useless products, manipulative marketing tactics, bad public policy, and poor decision making. The pressure to succumb to these things seems relentless, draining energy every time you turn on the television, read a newspaper, or pause to watch the world go around.

Most of us can't change the big picture. We only have influence over a small corner of the world, our small picture. We can't keep others from making bad choices about infants and toddlers, but we can make sure the choices we make are good. We can choose to be thoughtful, we can choose cardboard boxes and sand over electronic teddy bears and obnoxiously loud "educational" toys, we can build strong emotional environments, we can be mindful and fully engage in the dance of early care and education, we can promote child-centered play, exploration, and discovery. We can choose to let infants and toddlers *be* infants and toddlers, not pushing their development but allowing it to unfold naturally and at their individual pace.

Our babies will grow up and live most of their lives in a world most of us can barely imagine. They will confront challenges we have not even envisioned. They will develop and use new technology about which we can only dream. Many will work at jobs that do not exist at this moment in industries that will be wholly new. I close my eyes and picture Brenden, Annie, Lilly, Siddha, and all the other babies who have crawled across my playroom floor as their generation leads the world fifty years from now. I hope they are still curious and eager to find answers. I hope they are as loving and kind as they are now. I hope they are joyful and smile easily.

Our babies currently reap the benefits of our good choices and, in the future, they will be responsible for dealing with our bad choices. They will need every bit of creativity, insight, ingenuity, cleverness, thoughtfulness, and originality they can muster to dream big and meet the challenges awaiting them. Right now, their powerful and bendy little brains are wiring themselves to meet those future challenges. As a caregiver, a professional role model, and a lab assistant, you have great influence over their development. You can choose to help them play, explore, and discover in warm spring rains. You can choose to act with thoughtfulness and intention. You can choose to respectfully nurture their natural development. You can choose to make the right choice over the easy choice in any given moment. Please make choices that help the infants and toddlers in your life thrive.

References

American Academy of Pediatrics. 1999. Policy statement: Media education. *Pediatrics* 104 (2): 341–43.

California Childcare Health Program. 2006. Instructor's guide: Quality in early care and education. Berkeley, CA: California Childcare Health Program. http://www.ucsfchildcarehealth.org/pdfs/Curricula/Instuctors_Guide/CCHA_IG_3_Quality_v5.pdf (accessed February 2, 2009).

Csíkszentmihályi, Mihaly. 1990. *Flow: The psychology of optimal experience.* New York: Harper and Row.

———. 1996. *Creativity: Flow and the psychology of discovery and invention.* New York: HarperCollins.

———. 1997. *Finding flow: The psychology of engagement with everyday life.* New York: Basic Books.

Dombro, Amy Laura, Laura J. Colker, and Diane Trister Dodge. 1999. *The Creative curriculum for infants and toddlers.* Bethesda, MD: Teaching Strategies, Inc.

Elkind, David. 2007. *The power of play: How spontaneous, imaginative activities lead to happier, healthier children.* Cambridge, MA: Da Capo Press.

Gerber, Magda, and Allison Johnson. 1997. *Your self-confident baby: How to encourage your child's natural abilities from the very start.* Hoboken, NJ: Wiley.

Golinkoff, Roberta Michnick, Kathy Hirsh-Pasek, and Diane Eyer. 2003. *Einstein never used flash cards: How our children really learn—and why they need to play more and memorize less.* Emmaus, PA: Rodale.

Greenman, Jim, Anne Stonehouse, and Gigi Schweikert. 2008. *Prime times.* St. Paul, MN: Redleaf Press.

Harlow, Harry F. 1958. The nature of love. *American Psychologist* 13:673–85.

Holt, John. 1989. *Learning all the time.* Reading, MA: Addison-Wesley.

Linn, Susan E. 2004. *Consuming kids: The hostile takeover of childhood.* New York: New Press.

Medina, J. 2008. *Brain rules: 12 principles for surviving and thriving at home, work, and school.* Seattle: Pear Press.

National Association of Child Care Resource and Referral Agencies. 2007. Recent rash of deaths in child care: Better standards, oversight, and training needed. Press release. June 15.

Rideout, Victoria J., Elizabeth A. Vandewater, and Ellen A. Wartella. 2003. *Electronic media in the lives of infants, toddlers, and preschoolers.* Menlo Park, CA: Henry J. Kaiser Family Foundation.

Sharples, Tiffany. 2007. Lifelong effects of childhood obesity. *Time,* December 7. http://www.time.com/time/health/article/0,8599,1692184,00.html.

Shore, R. 1997. *Rethinking the brain: New insights into early development.* New York: Families and Work Institute.

Thomas, Susan Gregory. 2007. *Buy, buy, baby: How consumer culture manipulates parents and harms young minds.* Boston: Houghton Mifflin.